INSIDER'S PLAYBOOK TO THE ART OF PERSUASION

Warmups And Drills To Develop Your Skills

Dr. Rick Kirschner
Ashland, Oregon, USA

Copyright © 2007 by Dr. Rick Kirschner. All rights reserved. Printed in the United States of America. Except as permitted under the United States Copyright Act of 1976, no part of this publication may be reproduced or distributed in any form or by any means, or stored in a database or retrieval system, without the prior written permission of the publisher.

ISBN: 978-0-6151-6216-4

Talk Natural Press
A Division of The Art of Change LLC

The Art of Change books and multimedia products are available at special quantity discounts to use as premiums and sales promotions, or for use in corporate training programs. For more information, please write to the Director of Special Sales, The Art of Change LLC, P.O. Box 896, Ashland, OR 97520. Or contact your local bookstore.

It's one thing to have a lofty idea. It's another thing entirely to bring that idea to fruition. This is where the rubber meets the road, where action speaks louder than words, where it's not what you know but what you do with what you know that counts. This is how to make your communication count.

For a better world, persuasion's the key.
This is where change begins.
Thank you for choosing the Playbook.
Now let's go score some wins!

TABLE OF CONTENTS

1. TABLE OF CONTENTS iv
2. INTRODUCTION 1
3. USEFUL DEFINITIONS 3
4. USEFUL ASSUMPTIONS 8
5. STAGES OF CHANGE 12
6. POSSIBLE OUTCOMES 18
7. THE ACCEPTANCE ZONE 21
8. BLEND TO BUILD TRUST 24
9. BLEND WITH NEED-STYLE 27
10. LISTEN TO GO DEEP 31
11. FIND THE MAP: MOTIVATION 35
12. MAP: ACCESS LANGUAGE 53
13. FIND THE MAP: POSITION 58
14. INFORMATION GATES 63
15. TRANSITIONAL OPENERS 77
16. ORGANIZING THEMES 87
17. DELIVERY GUIDES 99
18. FUNNY PERSUASION 109
19. SEVEN SIGNALS INTRODUCTION 118
20. THE SIGNAL OF AFFINITY 119
21. THE SIGNAL OF COMPARISON 123
22. THE SIGNAL OF CONFORMITY 129
23. THE SIGNAL OF RECIPROCITY 132
24. THE SIGNAL OF AUTHORITY 135
25. THE SIGNAL OF CONSISTENCY 141

TABLE OF CONTENTS (Continued)

26. **THE SIGNAL OF SCARCITY** 145
27. **QUESTIONS? OBJECTIONS?** 148
28. **DEALING WITH OPPOSITION** 156
29. **CLOSING** 162
30. **PRESENCE** 165
31. **AND IN CONCLUSION** 168
32. **BIBLIOGRAPHY** 172
33. **ABOUT THE AUTHOR** 173

INTRODUCTION

The Rules of Art

Why a Playbook? It's the right thing to do. The Insider's Guide To The Art Of Persuasion is a collection of skills, strategies, cues and clues that you can use for the purpose of positive change. The materials in the Guide are organized for easy absorption and application. But it's a concentrated brew. It would take me a full twenty days of training to teach all these skills to you in a way that let's you play in as powerful a way as possible. So I've created this Playbook with the intention of helping you to help yourself.

You know the saying: The proof is in the pudding. Well the truth of this work is in the doing. No matter what you think the words mean, until you have tested an idea you will not truly know how it works. The Insider's Playbook is designed as a self-paced learning program. I recommend that you only go as far as the exercise or activity in front of you. Then do that. Then do that all the way through to the end of the book. From that point on, the plays in the Playbook will be yours to use as you like for as long as you like.

INSIDER'S PLAYBOOK

I've left space after certain questions for you to write down your answers. I recommend, however, that you get yourself a notebook or a journal, and write your answers to Playbook questions in there. That way you will be able to use the Playbook again and again.

REGARDING EXAMPLES: I've done my best to provide examples so as to clarify my meaning on key ideas. You will find a consistent product example, service example, and an idea example used throughout the book. You can read all the examples, one of them or none of them. In truth, the most important piece is that you do the activity or exercise. Then you will understand what it means to practice the art of persuasion. And you will know why persuasion is the most powerful change art of all.

Play by play, I'm going to take you through the doors and past the curtains to the inside of the art of persuasion. You have a clear view, so no need to crane your neck. And please, no holding your breath, either. The skills are all here, and learning them is simple and easy, so long as you go step by step. Relax. Take it all in. Have some fun. Find out what's possible. Then, when you let go and open up to the possibilities of the moment, you will see for yourself and hear for yourself and think for yourself and discover how you really feel about how the magic is done and the game is played with the Insider's Guide To The Art Of Persuasion.

1
USEFUL DEFINITIONS

The purpose of this chapter is to create a shared frame of reference for understanding the Rules of Art in the Art of Persuasion. Your purpose in answering these questions is to gain insight into how influence and persuasion apply to you.

Write your answers below:

1. INFLUENCE
What does **INFLUENCE** mean to you?

Who has it? How do they use it?

How do you already use your influence?

2. NEGATIVE INFLUENCE
What are the negative influences in your life?

3. PEER PRESSURE

In what situations do you go along with the crowd? Why? How do you take on the characteristics of the people in that crowd? Where else?

4. LIMITED INPUTS

Where do you get your news? How do you consistently read a paper? What kind of shows do you watch on TV? What do you listen to on the radio? Where do you get books to read? What kind of books do you read?

What aren't you reading, listening to, and watching that might give you a more informed perspective? What is one action you can take right now to broaden the scope of your inputs?

5. COERCION

Does anyone have coercive power in your life? Who is it? What gives them that power? What does it cost them?

Do you exercise coercive power with others? Who? Why? What is your desired outcome? What does it cost you?

USEFUL ASSUMPTIONS

6. BEHAVIOR SERVES A PURPOSE

What are the motivations behind your most successful behaviors? What are the motivations behind your most problematic behaviors? Assuming that behavior serves purpose, why do you do those behaviors? What do you seek to accomplish?

7. ASSUME THE POSITION
(PICK ONE ANSWER FOR EACH QUESTION)
Are you for the war or against the war?
Are you pro-choice or pro-life?
Do you think that the environment should be considered over special or private interests, or the reverse?
Should the United Nations have more power or less power in the affairs of nations?
Are you progressive, conservative, libertarian or green?
Should employees do what they're told because employers see the big picture, or should employers listen to their employees because they have a better sense of what's actually going on?
Are you pro-business or pro-labor?
Which is better, chocolate or vanilla?
Which is better, healthy food or a healthy appetite?
Why do you care about any of this at all?

INSIDER'S PLAYBOOK

8. MANIPULATION

Are you afraid of being manipulated? By whom? Where? When? About what? Based on what you read in this chapter of the book, what can you do to protect yourself from manipulation?

Are you afraid of being manipulative? Who are you afraid of manipulating? Why? Based on what you read in the book or heard in the audio program, what is one thing you must take into account in order to have integrity in your persuasion efforts?

USEFUL ASSUMPTIONS

9. PERSUASION PROPOSITION:

Who do you intend to persuade?
EXAMPLE: I intend to persuade you.

What you want them to do, think, decide?
EXAMPLE: I want you to use solar energy in your home, vibrational exercise for your body, and to do the activities in this Playbook for the Insider's Guide To The Art Of Persuasion.

Where do you intend to persuade them?
EXAMPLE: In the pages of this Playbook

When do you intend to persuade them?
 EXAMPLE: While you are reading the examples

Why do you want to persuade?
EXAMPLE: Change for the better is the mission of my business. All three of my persuasion propositions will have meaningful and lasting benefits for you, the reader, which fulfills my mission.

Why will your persuadee want you to succeed?
EXAMPLE: Values. Rewards. Challenge. Esteem. Purpose. Other.

2

USEFUL ASSUMPTIONS

1. GIVE UP THE NEED TO BE RIGHT
What limiting assumptions do you have about the people in your life, the people you work for, the people you work with, and the people you deal with on a regular basis? List three examples here.

Hint: Whatever you assume to be true, you act like it's true and look for proof. So a limiting assumption is something you get to be right about that isn't getting you a result that you want. Just identify results you're getting that you don't want, or areas of predictable conflict, and you'll find limiting assumptions behind them.

LIMITING ASSUMPTION:

LIMITING ASSUMPTION:

LIMITING ASSUMPTION:

USEFUL ASSUMPTIONS

2. YOU CANNOT NOT INFLUENCE PEOPLE
Identify three situations today where you influenced someone's response, through a question that you asked, or a statement that you made. What were the questions? What were the statements? If you can't think of your own examples, identify three situations where someone else influenced the response.

3. QUESTIONS HAVE PERSUASIVE POWER
Identify one question that you could have asked of someone today to set an expectation, expose motivation or intent, invite thought, introduce options, or take a conversation down a different path?

4. FLEXIBILITY INCREASES ABILITY
Name one thing that happened today that you thought or felt or reacted to as unacceptable. What else could it have meant? Where might it have been a good thing? How could it have been useful?

INSIDER'S PLAYBOOK

5. RESISTANCE IS A RESULT
Provide one example of you insisting that something happen a certain way, or someone agree with you? Provide one example of you telling someone or selling someone on your idea or information, or where you poured out your words like a fire hose instead of listening, caring and then sharing. If you can't think of any examples, then notice this behavior in others, and record what you noticed here.

6. OUR OWN INTERESTS PERSUADE US
Why should someone care about your persuasion proposition? What's in it for them to listen to you? Respond to you? Take your desired action?

7. BEGIN WITH THE END IN MIND
Time to revisit your persuasion proposition.

What do you propose to do? (This is your idea, solution, product or service.)

Who do you want to persuade to do it?

Where do you intend for this to happen?

When do you intend for this to happen?

Why do you want to persuade your persuadee?

Why will they care?

USEFUL ASSUMPTIONS

REVIEW: USEFUL ASSUMPTIONS

YOU CANNOT NOT INFLUENCE PEOPLE.
EXPLAIN:

QUESTIONS HAVE PERSUASIVE POWER.
EXPLAIN:

FLEXIBILITY INCREASES ABILITY.
EXPLAIN:

RESISTANCE IS A RESULT.
EXPLAIN:

OUR OWN INTERESTS PERSUADE US.
EXPLAIN:

BEGIN WITH THE END IN MIND.
EXPLAIN:

3

STAGES OF CHANGE

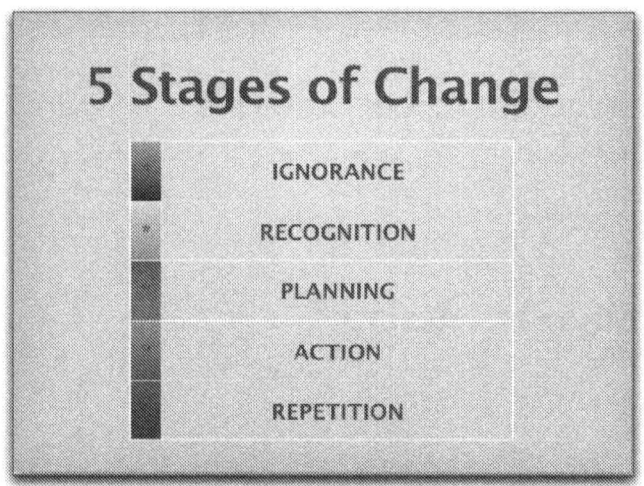

Stage one is IGNORANCE.

Assume that your persuadee is ignorant of the benefits or reasons for your proposition unless you have specific evidence to the contrary. The question is, ignorant of what? And of what kind?

POSSIBLE OUTCOMES

PRODUCT EXAMPLE: What do you know about vibrational exercise?

SERVICE EXAMPLE: What do you know about solar power for your home provided as a service?

IDEA EXAMPLE: What experience do you have with learning through the doing of exercises in a Playbook like this one?

YOUR TURN:

If Willful or Ignorant of Consequences:

How can you create a context of receptivity, to make it comfortable for your persuadee before introducing behaviorally-specific information? Write down your ideas here.

EXAMPLE: The three examples I use in this Playbook (PRODUCT, SERVICE, IDEA) are meant to give you tangible reference points for learning the patterns and strategies in The Insider's Guide To The Art Of Persuasion. You do not have to purchase anything in order to benefit from the examples I provide in this book. Nor do you have to believe the things I tell you, although I promise to tell you the truth to the best of my ability. All that I ask of you is to consider the examples as examples, in order to help you learn. Does that work for you?

YOUR TURN:

If ignorant of what to do about a known problem:

What available options and methods can you bring to your persuadee's attention?

PRODUCT EXAMPLE: I can provide you with examples of each persuasion proposition. I can send you to a website with lots of research data on V.E.

SERVICE EXAMPLE: I can show you a video of a famous actor who is advocating for the solar service.

IDEA EXAMPLE: I can let you read testimonials from students of mine who have done the exercises in this book and found them remarkably beneficial.

YOUR TURN:

If ignorant of why it matters:

What motivational information can you provide that speaks to your persuadee's interests, values or sense of purpose?

PRODUCT EXAMPLE: Do you want to be fit and healthy? Then you should learn all you can about V.E.

SERVICE EXAMPLE: Would you like to live in a healthier environment, and help wean your country from the oil economy that is contributing to geopolitical instability? Then you owe it to yourself to consider solar power for your home.

POSSIBLE OUTCOMES

IDEA EXAMPLE: Do you want to actually learn the skills offered to you in The Insider's Guide To The Art Of Persuasion? Only by taking some kind of action to internalize what you've read or heard can you succeed at becoming a masterful persuader.

YOUR TURN:

Stage Two is RECOGNITION

What questions does your persuadee have about your proposition? Or might have once you've brought them to this stage?

PRODUCT EXAMPLE: How much does a Jiggler cost? What kind of guarantee does it come with? What kind of research do you have to back up your health claims? Where can I get one? How long does it take to get it? How does the affiliate program work?

SERVICE EXAMPLE: How much for the solar power? How is it provided? Who pays if something goes wrong? How can I obtain this service?

IDEA EXAMPLE: How many people have actually tried the Insider's Guide To The Art Of Persuasion program successfully? How do you know it works? How long do the skills last?

YOUR TURN:

INSIDER'S PLAYBOOK

Stage Three is PLANNING

What are the specific action steps required for your proposition to happen?

PRODUCT EXAMPLE: Step one: Learn about the Jiggler. Step two: Order the Jiggler. Step three. Use the Jiggler for 10 minutes a day.

SERVICE EXAMPLE: Step one: Learn about the solar system being offered. Step two: Get your name on the list to lock in your current energy rate. Step three. Wait until the build out comes to your area.

IDEA EXAMPLE: Step one: Read the activity. Step two: Do the activity in a safe learning environment. Step three: Try it out in the real world.

YOUR TURN:

First step:

Second step:

Third step:

Stage Four is ACTION

How can you support your persuadee in this stage? What encouragement can you provide? What reassurances can you offer? What feedback can you make available to make sense of what happens?

PRODUCT EXAMPLE: Follow up phone call or email after product delivery. Regular sessions with me or someone else as a coach. Answer any questions as they arise.

POSSIBLE OUTCOMES

SERVICE EXAMPLE: Updates on the build out. Answer any questions as they arise.

IDEA EXAMPLE: Checklist in each chapter. Summaries when appropriate. Regular sessions with me or someone else as a coach. Teleconference. Membership group (Change Artist Guild).

YOUR TURN:

Stage Five is REPETITION

What opportunities exist for the repetition of a desired behavior? Or to revisit and reinforce your proposition as it unfolds?

PRODUCT EXAMPLE: Create a reminder on my calendar to follow up with customer every three months.

SERVICE EXAMPLE: Regular updates via email until design and installation are complete. Then point to savings at the end of each year, along with an accounting of how much oil wasn't used as the result of your installation and total company build out to date.

IDEA EXAMPLE: Sign up for my free newsletter, read my blog, listen to my podcast, and make it part of your weekly or monthly routine. Begin immediately. Once you've subscribed to my ENEWS, you'll receive regular reminders to act on what you've learned.
YOUR TURN:

POSSIBLE OUTCOMES

Have fun with this section, and don't skip past it. This is a big deal. Outcomes = Results.

Parallel

You say to-may-to, I say to-mah-to, and we agree to disagree (or simply disagree.)

How could you intentionally create this result with your persuadee? What kinds of behaviors would you engage in if you wanted to guarantee that nothing changes?

Polarize

You say to-may-to, I say to-mah-to, and we both wish the tomatoes were rotten so we had something to throw at each other. Let's call the whole thing off!

How could you intentionally create this result with your persuadee? What kind of behaviors would you engage in if you wanted to guarantee that both you and your persuadee end up farther apart than had you left well enough alone?

POSSIBLE OUTCOMES

Merge

I say to-may-to, you say to-mah-to, and we both realize that we're saying the same thing with a different accent! Let's enjoy whatever it is together!

How could you intentionally create this result with your persuadee? What kind of behaviors would you engage in if you wanted to guarantee that both you and your persuadee recognize the value of each other's motivations and intentions?

Persuade

I say to-may-to, and you say, ok, to-may-to it is.

How could you intentionally create this result with your persuadee? What kind of behaviors would you engage in if you wanted to guarantee that your persuadee comes around to your point of view, where your intentions become their intentions, your position becomes their position, your motivation becomes their motivation? (Just guess. Don't worry. The rest of this book will help you answer this question specifically!)

INSIDER'S PLAYBOOK

SUMMARY:

Based on what you've come up with in answer to the questions in this chapter, what do you want to be certain NOT TO DO in your efforts to be more persuasive?

What do you want to be certain TO DO in your efforts to be more persuasive?

5

THE ACCEPTANCE ZONE

You must first seek not to persuade, but to build a relationship of trust. To achieve the result of greater trust, you must be trustworthy. And to be trustworthy, you must have your persuadee's best interests (as they understand them, not as you desire them,) in your mind, your heart and in your actions. Read the chapter or listen to the track, then answer these questions. **Answers are at the end of the chapter.**

1. Name the three receiving zones.

2. Which receiving zone contains your persuadee's MAP of reality?

3. The MAP consists of _____,

_____, and _____.

4. How many possible MAPs of reality are there surrounding your persuadee's MAP of reality as pertains to your proposition?

5. If your proposition winds up in the "I don't care" zone, you should:
a. Panic
b. Turn away in apathy
c. Stop talking and start listening

6. To help people to accept positive change, the first step is to understand what they have to _ _ _ _ by changing, or _ _ _ _ by staying the same.

7. The size of a person's Acceptance zone is determined by:
a. Self-identity and self-definition
b. Investment of their time and thought
c. Attractiveness of your proposal
d. All of the above

8. Your opposition to their MAP guarantees their _____ to your proposition.

Why do you think this is?

8. If a person has enough _____ in you, you're already in their acceptance zone.

THE ACCEPTANCE ZONE

ANSWERS:
1. Acceptance, Rejection, Uncommitted
2. Acceptance Zone
3. Motivation, Access Language, Position
4. An infinite number
5. C
6. GAIN, LOSE
7. d
8. Resistance
9. Trust

6

BLEND TO BUILD TRUST

Answers at the end of the chapter

1. All the other skills and strategies in this book /audio program depend on _____ to be effective.
Explain:

2. Blending means to _____ differences and send _____ of _____.
What are some of the differences between you and your persuadee?

3. Who are some of the people with whom you already have positive relationships and trust? What is the common ground on which you've built those relationships?

BLEND TO BUILD TRUST

Basic Rule

Nobody cooperates with anybody who seems to be against them.

4. The key words in this rule are _____.

5. In every interaction, every person looks and listens for an answer to one. What is that question?

6. What do the 55, 38 and 7 represent?

7. How can you reduce the differences between yourself and your persuadee using the 55%?
Elaborate here.

8. How can you reduce the differences between yourself and your persuadee using the 38%?
Elaborate here.

INSIDER'S PLAYBOOK

ANSWERS:

1. Blending
2. Reduce differences, send signals of similarity
4. seems to be
5. Are you with me?
6. 55% what you see, 38% what you hear, 7% what is said
7. Blend with body posture, facial expressions, animation
8. Blend with voice tone, tempo, volume, pitch, timbre

7

BLEND WITH NEED-STYLE

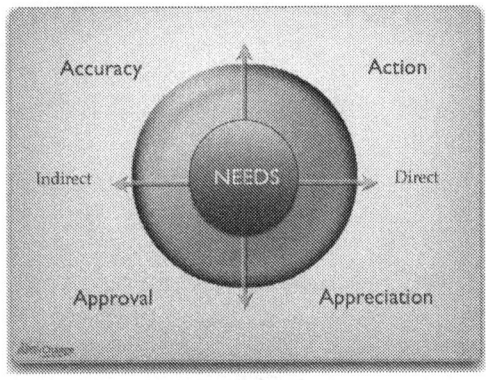

Answers are at the end of the chapter.

1. Describe the difference between personality and behavior, and which one is more important to the art of persuasion.

2. Dr. Rick's version of 'Think outside the box," is:

3. There are how many styles of communication in the

INSIDER'S PLAYBOOK

Need-Style model?
a. Four
b. Hundreds and hundreds.
c. Thousands and thousands.
d. An infinite number

4. The two variables that form the Need-Style grid are _____ and _____.

5. The two relevant components of a TASK are _____ _____ and _____s.

6. The two relevant components of PEOPLE are _____ and _____.

7. When a person is focused on the end result of an interaction or an idea, he has a communication need for _____.
How does this person speak? Elaborate.

How would you talk with this person?

8. When a person is focused on the details of an interaction or an idea, she has a communication need for _____.
How does this person speak? Elaborate.

How would you talk with this person?

BLEND WITH NEED-STYLE

9. When a person is focused more on what others think and say than on her own thoughts and feelings, she has a need for _____.
How does this person speak? Elaborate.

How would you talk with this person?

10. When a person is focused more on her own thoughts and feelings than the thoughts and feelings of others, she has a need for _____.
How does this person speak? Elaborate.

How would you talk with this person?

INSIDER'S PLAYBOOK

ANSWERS:

1. Personality is a generalization based on limited information. Behavior is fluid. It changes depending on who, what, where and when. Personality is, in effect, an opinion. Opinions by their very nature lock out nonconforming details. Behavior is observable, and predictable.

2. Don't get in the box.

3. a

4. Focus of Attention, Assertiveness Level.

5. End result, Details

6. Self, Others

7. Action; Direct and to the point, Bottom line

8. Accuracy; Indirect and detailed, step by step

9. Approval; Indirect and considerate, friendly, helpful

10. Appreciation; Direct and elaborate, with enthusiasm

8

LISTEN TO GO DEEP

1. What are the three phases of persuasion?

Phase One _____

Phase Two _____

Phase Three _____

1. Words are:
    a. Symbols for experience
    b. The tip of the iceberg of meaning
    c. An opportunity to go deeper
    d. All of the above

3. When people talk, what do they always want?

4. True or false.
People actually like to hear themselves talk.

5. Information is _____.

INSIDER'S PLAYBOOK

6. True or false.
When listening, it is important to look and sound like you completely understand.

7. BACKTRACKING means:

8. The time to look confused is when:
   a. People make no sense
   b. You are asking a question
   c. When you are confused
   d. When you don't understand

9. Always _____ before asking a question.

10. Open ended questions always begin with 'who, what, where, when, why and how.' Why isn't 'why' one of the open-ended questions that you ask when first seeking to understand?

11. What three words can you say when you don't know what question to ask?

12. You cannot reason with an _____ person. But you can get an _____ person to become reasonable.

LISTEN TO GO DEEP

13. Actively listening is useful when
    a. A person doesn't know what they're talking about
    b. You suspect a hidden agenda
    c. You suspect someone is lying
    d. You think it is a bad idea
    e. When dealing with criticism
    f. All of the above

14. Actively listening results in one of three possible outcomes when dealing with criticism. What are they?

INSIDER'S PLAYBOOK

ANSWERS:
1. Listen, Transition, Talk

2. d

3. to be heard and understood

4. True

5. Information is persuasive power.

6. True

7. Say back what someone says using the same words

8. b

9. backtrack

10. Most people don't even know what they're talking about (tip of the iceberg), When you ask why before what, who, where and when, they may be inclined to make something up. Why questions complicate when asked too soon.

11. Tell me more.

12. Upset, upset

13. f

14. The person realizes it isn't about you. You learn something useful. It takes all the fun out of it for the person trying to poke at you.

9

FIND THE MAP: MOTIVATION

FEAR AND DESIRE

1. Identify three things you've been motivated to do or change in your life at any time in the past because of a desire. What did you do or change? What was the desire that motivated you to do it?

2. Identify three things you've been motivated to do or not do, change or not change, because of fear. What did you do or change, not do or not change? What were you afraid of?

3. Have you ever gotten a speeding ticket? Or been in trouble anywhere for any reason? What was the incident? What did you learn from it? How has this affected your life?

4. What is something you want to change in your life right now? Why? Is it fear or desire or both? Elaborate.

MASLOW'S HEIRARCHY

5. On a scale of 1 to 10, with 10 being the highest, how much motivation do you have in your life, right now, to eat, sleep, be comfortable? What does this motivation cause you to do?

6. On a scale of 1 to 10, with 10 being the highest, how much motivation do you have in your life, right now, to be safe and secure? What does this motivation cause you to do?

7. On a scale of 1 to 10, with 10 being the highest, how much motivation do you have in your life, right now, to belong to groups?

8. On a scale of 1 to 10, with 10 being the highest, how much motivation do you have in your life, right now, to take on responsibility, or have the respect and esteem of others? What does this motivation cause you to do?

FIND THE MAP: MOTIVATION

9. How much motivation do you have in your life, right now, to fulfill your potential? How much of a role does this play in your life? How much time do you give to this each day?

10. Based on your answers to Questions 5-9, what can you observe about the role these motivations play in your daily life?

MCCLELLAND'S MOTIVATIONAL MODEL

David McClelland developed another model while teaching at Harvard. He believed that each of us exhibits some combination of these 3 motivations in our work.

Use these descriptions to make an assessment of yourself. On a percentage basis, rate yourself in your work based on these three motivations.

A person motivated by the need for achievement seeks opportunities for advancement, and works to attain challenging goals, and gets feedback about their progress and successes. He or she may fall into the trap of asking too much of others in the mistaken belief that everyone shares this motivation.

RATE YOURSELF: (98% of my work motivation)

EXPLAIN:

A person motivated by the need for authority seeks opportunities for influence, status and prestige. They eagerly take charge and they make strong commitments. Their downfall is getting attached to an idea, or lacking the skills to get others to act.

RATE YOURSELF: (98% of my work motivation)

EXPLAIN:

A person motivated by the need for affiliation wants to be liked, and works really hard at it. Appreciated by many, disliked by a few, the need to be liked gets in the way of decisive action.

RATE YOURSELF: (98% of my work motivation)

EXPLAIN:

KIRSCHNER'S MOTIVATIONAL MODEL

According to the Kirschner model, there are six motivational sets, each with a TOWARDS side and an AWAY side. These sets play an important role in the choices people make.

Rather than having one set of motivations for everything you do, you have different motivations for different situations and activities. Your motivations depend on where you are, who you're with, and what matters most to you in that context. The fastest way to understand motivation in others is to understand your own motivations first.

FIND THE MAP: MOTIVATION

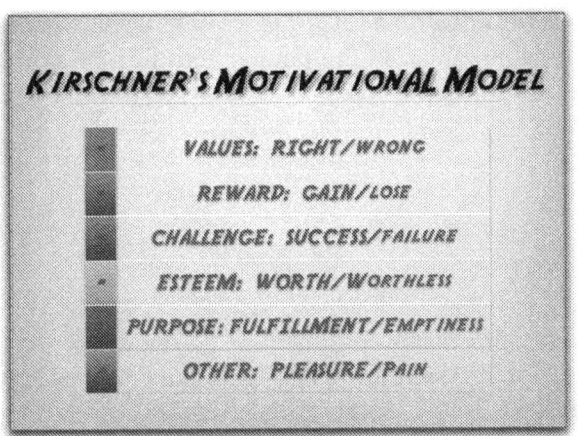

VALUES

Give an example of something you've done, are doing, or plan to do based on what you perceive as the right thing to do.

Then give an example of something you've done or not done, are doing or not doing, or plan to do or not to do, because of what you perceive as the wrong thing to do, or not to do. What is the value? What is important to you about that?

REWARD

Give an example of something you've done, are doing, or plan to do, in order to get a reward of some kind. Is the reward intrinsic or extrinsic?

INSIDER'S PLAYBOOK

Give an example of something you've done or not done, are doing or not doing, or plan to do or not to do, in order to avoid a punishment. Is the punishment intrinsic or extrinsic?

CHALLENGE

Give an example of something you've done, are doing, or plan to do, for the sake of a challenge, and the potential to succeed at it. Is this something involving other people in order to meet the challenge, or something that requires only you?

Give an example of something you've done or not done, are doing or not doing, or plan to do or not to do, in order to avoid failure.

ESTEEM

Give an example of something you've done, are doing, or plan to do, in order to enhance your reputation, or be valued and appreciated by others.

Give an example of something you've done or not done, are doing or not doing, or plan to do or not to do, in order to avoid shame or dishonor.

FIND THE MAP: MOTIVATION

PURPOSE

Give an example of something you've done, are doing, or plan to do, that offers you no material benefit or compensation, in order to fulfill your sense of purpose.

Give an example of something you've done or not done, are doing or not doing, or plan to do or not to do, in order to prevent or eliminate a sense of emptiness in your life.

OTHER

Give an example of something you've done, are doing, or plan to do, in order to experience pleasure.

Give an example of something you've done or not done, are doing or not doing, or plan to do or not to do, in order to prevent, avoid or eliminate pain.

KIRSCHNER'S MODEL AND YOUR PROPOSITION

VALUES

Now, what makes your persuasion proposition the right thing for your persuadee to do, and what makes the failure to adopt it the wrong thing for your persuadee to do?

PRODUCT EXAMPLE: Why is vibrational exercise the right thing to do? Because taking care of yourself while you can means you won't become a burden to your family as you age.

SERVICE EXAMPLE: Why is using the service of solar energy for your home the right thing to do? Because you as an individual can actually do something to put an end to all the problems caused by global addiction to oil. Because your children deserve a better world.

IDEA EXAMPLE: Why is doing the activities in this Playbook the right thing to do? Because otherwise you have wasted your investment of money and time. It's wrong to waste either when both are so precious. And, more importantly, because some day, something important may actually depend on you! You've got to be prepared to be persuasive, so you can do the right thing if and when you are called on to do so!

YOUR TURN:

FIND THE MAP: MOTIVATION

REWARD

PRODUCT EXAMPLE: Rewards from using the Jiggler? You can free up your time, since it only takes 10 minutes a day to get the muscle tone equivalent of 90 minutes at the gym. Your clothes will fit better. You will feel more vital and alive. And the company has an affiliate program that pays you when people buy the product on your recommendation. What do you lose if you don't use the Jiggler? You lose precious time. Unless you're committed to exercise, the older you get, the more body functions are at risk for deterioration over time.

SERVICE EXAMPLE: Rewards from using solar power for your home? Intrinsic reward of knowing you are helping to solve the serious problems facing the human race. The extrinsic reward of locking in the rate you're currently paying for energy, no matter how much energy rates increase over the next 25 years.

IDEA EXAMPLE: Intrinsic reward of the confidence that comes from preparation. Extrinsic reward of building stronger relationships, gaining influence and prestige, being able to get what you want!

YOUR TURN:

CHALLENGE

How might you present your proposition as an exciting or worthwhile challenge for your persuadee?

PRODUCT EXAMPLE: I challenge you to find a better or easier-to-use piece of equipment than the V.E. that can deliver these kinds of results in so little time.

SERVICE EXAMPLE: I challenge you to find a better or easier way to end our energy dependence on the oil economy, and cut off funding for conflict and terrorism.

LEARNING EXAMPLE: To acquire new skills is a big challenge. The number one cause of failure to learn is a failure to try. Yet you have learned new skills. You've met this challenge successfully in your life. You learned by doing. Not doing leads to failure. Doing leads to success. I challenge you to rise to the occasion, find the focus needed to do these exercises and succeed at what you've begun.

YOUR TURN:

FIND THE MAP: MOTIVATION

ESTEEM

Give an example of how your persuasion proposition serves the esteem needs of your persuadee.

PRODUCT EXAMPLE: How good you look and feel when you're toned and fit, instead of out of shape, feeling old and tired.

SERVICE EXAMPLE: How you feel about yourself knowing that you are part of the solution instead of part of the problem.

IDEA EXAMPLE: Being an insider instead of an outsider.

YOUR TURN:

INSIDER'S PLAYBOOK

PURPOSE

How might your persuasion proposition help fulfill your persuadee's sense of purpose in life?

PRODUCT EXAMPLE: You want to set a great example of taking care of yourself for your children and/or spouse.

SERVICE EXAMPLE: A better world is at the heart of all human endeavors, from science to philosophy, to religion, to business. Here is a business that gives the individual a way to do their part to bring that about!

IDEA EXAMPLE: It's time to raise your game, to be more of a player and participant in the events going on around you every day.

YOUR TURN:

FIND THE MAP: MOTIVATION

OTHER

How can your persuasion proposition give your persuadee pleasure? How can it help your persuadee avoid pain?

PRODUCT EXAMPLE: What a delightful way to begin each day, standing on the V.E. for ten minutes, staring out a window perhaps, and lining up your daily activities in your mind's eye before actually taking anything on. The pleasure of motion, of circulation, of a sense of aliveness. Avoiding the pain of bone density loss and possible osteoporosis that afflicts so many of the elderly; of a loss of equilibrium that eventually leads to elderly people falling down and breaking hips, arms and legs; of hormonal insufficiency and the emotional consequences that tear apart so many relationships; of the inability to get around like you used to be able to do.

SERVICE EXAMPLE: The pleasure of knowing that your energy rate will never increase as long as you subscribe to the service. The pleasure of knowing that you're using a renewable resource, thus leaving more resources to future generations. The pleasure of not having to deal with maintenance and permits and all the other hassles that go with owning your own solar system.

IDEA EXAMPLE: The pleasure of knowing what to say and when to say it; Of having your ideas adopted more often; of being in front of a change instead of dragged along behind it. Avoiding the pain of rejection, of hurt feelings, of not being able to stop a bad idea from winning out over a better one.

YOUR TURN:

INSIDER'S PLAYBOOK

STACKING THE MOTIVATIONAL DECK

Identify something that you want to do that requires a great deal of motivation on your part in order to make it happen.

EXAMPLE: Create an audio program, book and workbook

YOUR TURN:

Using Kirschner's Motivational Model, identify a motivation of each type, either towards or away or both.

VALUES:

Why is it right to do this?

EXAMPLE: Empower people working for positive change.
YOUR TURN:

Why is it wrong not to do it?
EXAMPLE: When good people do nothing, evil triumphs.
YOUR TURN:

REWARD:
What do you stand to gain as a reward for doing it?
Example: The satisfaction of a job well done.

What do you stand to lose if you don't do it?
Example: Very busy. Window of opportunity will close.

FIND THE MAP: MOTIVATION

ESTEEM:

How will doing this enhance your reputation or esteem in the opinion of others?

EXAMPLE: Bigger repertoire. Adds to my track record.
YOUR TURN:

How will not doing it undermine your reputation or esteem in the opinion of others?
EXAMPLE: Old news, out of sight, out of mind.
YOUR TURN:

CHALLENGE:

How will doing this help you to succeed in your life?
EXAMPLE: The more I achieve, the more I believe I can achieve.
YOUR TURN:

How will not doing it contribute to your failure in life?
EXAMPLE: I would doubt myself, and doubt could undo me. I might start to question all my commitments. I might hesitate to take anything if it was difficult.
YOUR TURN:

PURPOSE:

What makes doing this fulfilling to you as a human being?
EXAMPLE: I live to serve.
YOUR TURN:

What would be left unfulfilled in you if you didn't do it?
EXAMPLE: A missed opportunity to make a difference.
YOUR TURN:

OTHER:

What pleasure will you experience by doing this?
EXAMPLE: The pleasure of finishing what I've started.
YOUR TURN:

What pain will you experience by not doing it?
EXAMPLE: It will eat away at me until it is done.
YOUR TURN:

Motivations change, depending on the specific goal, objective, desire or fear. In this context, which of these motivations is the strongest for you, or matters most? Which of these motivations is the weakest, or matters least? Which of these motivations require more attention and development on your part in order to fully understand them?

TALK ABOUT IT HERE:

FIND THE MAP: MOTIVATION

Now, place these motivations in a stack, by order of importance for you. Put the most important motivation on the bottom of the stack, as support for the layer above it. Once you've prioritized, read the motivations from the top down, and then the bottom up, and notice how each effects your overall motivation to take action.

WEAKEST MOTIVATION

STRONGEST MOTIVATION

INSIDER'S PLAYBOOK

FIND OUT WHY

Find a partner who is willing to talk with you about his or her own motivations. Ask them the following questions.

Where do you have a lot of motivation in your life?

What do you like about that part of your life?

Why do you like that part of your life?

Where do you lack motivation in your life?

What don't you like about not having motivation in that part of your life?

Why don't you like not having motivation in that part of your life?

Why is that important to you? (Or NOT important to you?)

SUGGESTION:

Invest the rest of this day watching, listening for, and asking about motivation.

Whenever there is something that you have to do or want to do, invest a little thinking time about your own motivation towards and away.

10

MAP: ACCESS LANGUAGE

Our sensory preferences determine the way we pay attention. They come across in the way we describe our experiences. Your goal in this chapter is to become more flexible in the use of access language, so that you can speak clearly, confidently and comfortably with anyone.

<u>**REHEARSAL:**</u> Repeat the following phrases three times.

Sight
I see what you mean. That looks possible. Can you shed a little more light on that for me? It's beginning to dawn on me! Don't keep me in the dark any longer! Sorry, my memory is a little cloudy today. I see a whole spectrum of possibilities. That's a shining example. What a bright idea!

If you can, add some sight words of your own:

Sound:
That's music to my ears. Your words ring true. All that jazz. I hear you, loud and clear. We can orchestrate this campaign. A little tune up and we're ready. We work together in perfect harmony. You are clearing up the static. Thanks for helping me get past the noise.

If you can, add some sound words of your own.

INSIDER'S PLAYBOOK

Feeling:
Can you handle this? Not too tough? A soft touch. I can't quite put my finger on it. I've got to hand it to you. I feel like success is within our reach. I don't want to put this on you. Together we can do the heavy lifting. It's hard to push ahead, but we can smooth the way. Iron out the wrinkles. We'll begin the drumbeat, and soon everyone will jump on board.

If you can, add some feeling words of your own.

Smell and Taste:
That's really sweet of you. Let's not end this on a sour note. We don't want to stay until the bitter end. Last one in is a rotten egg. Whatever we do, it should be in the best possible taste. Give it to me in plain vanilla. Too bland? What a delicious idea! That's good food for thought. Let me chew on this for a while. I'd like time to digest what was said. That went down well.

If you can, add some smell and taste words of your own.

Unspecified Language

Unspecified language consists of words and phrases that you are likely to find in the verbal expressions of the cerebral and objectively trained - such as educators and scientists.

Let's be cautious. I'm confident we can develop this. I'm determined to persevere. I remain hopeful we can resolve this. I'm optimistic! I'm puzzled. I'm relieved. That is very thoughtful. It has yet to be decided.

If you can, add a few unspecified words of your own.

FIND THE MAP: ACCESS LANGUAGE

DISCOVER YOUR OWN SENSORY PREFERENCES

1. Write a description of your day, starting with the moment you woke up, paying attention to the visual component of the experience. What did you see? How did it look? Do your best to pay attention ONLY to the visual aspect of your day.

2. Write a description of your day, starting with the moment you woke up, paying attention to the hearing or auditory component of the experience. What did you hear? How did it sound? What did you say to yourself? What did your internal voice sound like?

3. Write a description of your day, starting with the moment you woke up, paying attention to the feeling or kinesthetic

component of the experience? What sensations did you experience? What emotions did you experience? How did these feelings feel? Where did you feel them?

4. Which of these descriptions came easiest to you? Which were the most difficult?

5. Attempt to describe your day, starting with the moment you woke up, without using any sensory language whatsoever.

<u>LISTENING TO OTHERS</u>

6. Spend 30 minutes today listening to others, and write down any sensory words or phrases that you hear.

7. Take a walk in nature. Near a pond. In a park. On a mountain. Write down everything you see, you hear and you feel.

FIND THE MAP: ACCESS LANGUAGE

YOUR PERSUASION PROPOSITION

8. Consider how you might emphasis each access language (Sight, Sound, Feeling, Unspecified) when describing your persuasion proposition to your persuadee.

PRODUCT EXAMPLE:

SIGHT – When you first look at the Vibrational Exerciser, you can see that it is a thing of beauty. The colorful and curved lines show you that the designers had a clear idea in mind of how this equipment should look in order to be aesthetically pleasing to the eye. Two sets of ten lights across show you your speed and elapsed time.

SOUND - The Vibrational Exerciser emits a pleasant quiet beeping sound when you start it up, and another beeping sound when a ten minute cycle is complete. I can tell you that I hear all the time about how this product speaks to a significant need in the lives of busy people. Their praise speaks volumes about how this equipment addresses their needs.

FEELING - When you step onto the Jiggler's platform, you can feel the surface bumps of the pad beneath your feet massaging your souls as the therapeutic vibrations work their way to the top of your head and back. The movement in your different muscle groups can be accentuated in the way you adjust your body posture.

UNSPECIFIED - This remarkable equipment delivers necessary improvements in the functionality of the human system. The workmanship is of the finest quality. And the benefits are significant.

YOUR TURN:

11

FIND THE MAP: POSITION

A position is a belief stated as a fact. Taking a position about someone's position is clearly not the solution. The real solution to dealing with positions is to introduce doubt, reframe meaning, or find out the interests behind positions and address those interests in new and creative ways. Persuasion happens when positions change.

STRONG POSITION

What is something that you believe strongly? How did you come to this belief? What makes you certain that it's true? Elaborate.

What part of this belief is the weakest part (i.e., You have the most uncertainty about it)?

Reframe this part. What else could it mean? What have you not considered or taken into account?

INFORMATION GATES

WEAK POSITION

What is something that you believe or believe in, but are not all that certain that its true?

What doubts do you have about it?   Elaborate.

What evidence do you need in order to have a stronger position?

What evidence would make your belief less believable to you?

INSIDER'S PLAYBOOK

OPPOSITION

Assume, for the moment, that your proposition might be met with opposition. What claim could be made that your proposition goes against something important to someone else? How might you make the claim that opposing your proposition undermines that same value? How could you make that claim in the form of a question?

PRODUCT EXAMPLE: I don't have time to exercise. Your Jiggler isn't something I'll use. When I'm done with work, I'm already hard pressed to find time for my family.

Response: If you don't take the time to do some kind of exercise, I'm concerned that for you it may be later than you think! Is it possible that the short ten minutes a day on the Jiggler will buy back your time from the time you waste because of illness and fatigue? When you are busy working, won't better circulation help you with sharper thinking so you can make better use of your time? Doesn't a healthier you mean give you more time with your family in the long run? Quality time, rather than sick time with them standing over you and worrying about you because you didn't take care of yourself?

SERVICE EXAMPLE: I've already looked into it, and I can't afford a solar system for my house. Your idea doesn't apply to me. I have to spend my money wisely.

Response: I see that. (access language) But I'm confused. Where is the wisdom in how you pay for power now? This system involves no system charges. No installation costs. No maintenance fees. And most importantly, no rate increases, so you would never pay more than you pay now for energy for the length of your contract. That certainly can't be said for the utility you pay now. So this system saves you money, and involves no out of pocket expense. How can you afford not to do this?

INFORMATION GATES

IDEA EXAMPLE: I've got your audio program. : I don't need to do any exercises to learn. I'm an auditory learner. I learn by listening. Your Playbook doesn't sound like something I need.

Response: I hear that. (access language) I also learn by listening. But I'm curious. How do you not need encouragement and support to do what you've heard to do? Do you mean to say that you hear and don't do, and call that learning? Does it help you to know that I designed these activities so that the Playbook is my voice giving you advice and encouragement that will help you to hear more and speak more persuasively? Do you think it is possible that the Playbook could help you to remember what you've heard, every time you try out an idea or apply a skill to something specific?

YOUR EXAMPLE:

RESPONSE:

OTHER QUESTIONS TO ANSWER

What questions might remain unanswered by your proposition as it stands now? How could you build the answers to those questions into your proposition?

Who might feel left out as a result of your proposition? How can you give them a role?

Who are the natural allies for your proposition? What opposition do they bring with them? What evidence can you provide that allies of your opposition might favor your proposition?

The Polarity Response
Who, if anyone, might oppose your proposition simply because it wasn't their own idea? How might you agree with their opposition, and put some of the ownership for your proposition on them?

Your Persuasion Proposition

12

INFORMATION GATES

In the English language, there are at least 9 information gates that separate surface structure from the deeper structure of meaning. These gates represent verbal expressions of limitations in the way people represent their own experiences to themselves.

The surface structure of a sentence is a generalization that leaves out much specific information. Every sentence gives you a variety of possible gates to drive through. You get to choose your gate, and your decision determines where you get to on the other side. If you pick a gate that yields little in the way of useful information, back up and try another one.

However, a warning is in order here. The questions presented in this chapter can also cause the gates to slam shut and stay closed forever! That is what will happen if you disobey the following three rules.

Rule #1. The way to know what someone means is to ask.

Rule #2: Blend with what you see and hear.

Rule #3: Backtrack before asking questions,

INSIDER'S PLAYBOOK

Gate 1: CONFUSION - Missing "W's".

Who, what, where, when.
Rule #4: There are always missing W's.
Question: Ask who, what, where, when specifically?

Pretend that a good friend of yours, someone you know really well, says, "I'm interested in people," and says it like it is obvious what that means. Your task here is to make a list of possible questions you could ask in order to find out all the missing "W's". Then answer each question, and question each answer until you have filled in as many of the four missing W's as possible. Double check. You may be amazed.

YOUR TURN: "I'm interested in people."
What don't you know?

INFORMATION GATES

Gate 2: INACTION - Vague Verbs

A verb is vague when it is missing a process.
Rule #5: All verbs are vague.
Rule #6: Always get the nouns before the verbs.
Question: How specifically?

Pretend that someone specific that you know says the following example statements to you. Your task is to make a list of possible questions you could ask, and then answer them as specifically as possible, in order to clarify the process, or how, of the following example statements.

EXAMPLE:
I'll get it done. (It = build a specific kind of widget)
Questions: How will you get it done?
Answer: I'll put it on my calendar.
Question: How will you get it done after you put it on your calendar?
Answer: I'll talk to the people involved and get their input.
Question: How will you get it done once you've gotten their input?
Answer: I'll connect A to B, then the A-B complex to C, until I have the entire widget assembled.

YOUR TURN:
"I'm interested in people."

INSIDER'S PLAYBOOK

Gate 3: STUCK - Freezer

A verb masquerading as a noun)
Question: How does (turn noun into verb) it happen?
A noun is a person, place or thing. A noun is tangible. A verb is a process word, and describes an action. A good way to learn about freezers is to practice making them! Freeze the following verbs into nouns and then use them in a sentence. Then ask the how question that thaws them out again.

<u>EXAMPLE</u>
Confuse - Your questions confuse me
Freezer: The result of your questions is confusion.
Question to thaw it out: How does my questioning confuse you?

<u>YOUR TURN:</u>
Disappoint - You disappoint me.
Freezer:
Question to thaw it out:

Afraid - I am afraid to fail.
Freezer:
Question to thaw it out:

Use - I use words in sentences.
Freezer:
Question to thaw it out:

Disgust - Your behavior disgusts me
Freezer:
Question to thaw it out:

Realize - I realize that you are new at this
Freezer:
Question to thaw it out:

INFORMATION GATES

Gate 4: INHIBITION - M.O.

Mode of operation: Limited by an obstacle or fear
Question: What stops you? (Ask for the obstacle) or
What would happen if you did? (Ask for the fear)
Limitation implies that there is no choice. What question would you ask in response to the following statements?

EXAMPLE: I can't do this right now.
Question: What would happen if you could?
Question: What stops you from doing it right now?

YOUR TURN:
I have to get out of here.
Question:

I must figure this out.
Question:

I should stop and take a break.
Question:

Now, make up a few examples of your own, along with possible questions.

1.

2.

3.

INSIDER'S PLAYBOOK

Gate 5: ABSTRACTION

Universal words (all or none)
Rule #7: Turn general into specific
Question: Who, what, where, when specifically?
A universal generalization is an easy gate to drive through. All you have to do is ask for the specific example of the generalization. If at first you don't succeed, you can escalate exaggeration to reveal the impossibility of what they are saying. When exaggerating, make sure that your non-verbal behavior is sending messages that you're on their side.

EXAMPLE: This will never work.
Question: Never work in what way? What would happen if it did?

YOUR TURN:
Everybody knows.
Question:

They always act like that.
Question:

There's no way I'm going in there.
Question:

EXAGGERATION PRACTICE:
This is an exercise in voice tone and energy. Take the abstracted statement, and escalate it three times, each time with more emphasis on the word, and ask for either an example or a counter example.
EXAMPLE: Everybody knows.
Everybody? Every single person? There isn't one person who doesn't know? There isn't one person anywhere who doesn't know? Not even one very small person?
YOUR TURN: It will never happen.
        Nobody is interested.
            You can always do better.

INFORMATION GATES

Gate 6: BLAME

As if X is the cause and Y is the Effect.
Rule #8: It's never about X. It's about the sensory cue that is interpreted as X.
Question: How does X cause Y?

A common way of disclaiming ownership over an unsavory result. Tease it apart by asking, "How does X cause Y specifically?" Backtrack as you disassemble the cause-effect relationship until you arrive at a sensory cue (see-hear-feel). Your task is to get the person to admit to being the cause of their own experience rather than the effect of circumstance.

EXAMPLE: 'He made me miss the turn.'
Question: How specifically did he make you miss the turn?
Answer: He kept talking when I was trying to read the signs.
Question: So his talking made you miss the turn?
Answer: Yes.
Question: Do you always miss the turn when people talk to you?
Answer: No.
Question? What happened this time?
Answer: I got distracted. Too many things on my mind.

Your turn:
'She made me forget what I was saying.'
Question:
Answer:
Question:
Answer:
Question:

'He wouldn't let me finish.'
Question:
Answer:
Question:
Answer:
Question:

INSIDER'S PLAYBOOK

Gate 7: EXCUSES

Implied Cause. Y? Because of X.
Rule #9: There is always a choice.
Question: How does X cause Y specifically?

A person implies a link between unrelated events. If X is true, then Y must follow. Or, if not for X, then Y would follow. The excuse sounds reasonable, and your mind is geared to accept it. Yet if you ask for the specific connection, quite often you'll find that the implied cause is just made up. Play this out a few times, and you'll find it difficult to hear an excuse the same way ever again.

EXAMPLE: I'd do that for you, but I'm busy on a project.
Question: How does being busy on that project prevent you from doing that for me?"

YOUR TURN: I'd help you out, but I have things to do.
Question:
Answer:
Question:

I'd consider it, but I'm up against a deadline.
Question:
Answer:
Question:

I'd love to tell you, but I gave my word.
Question:
Answer:
Question:

I would have finished it, but the phone kept ringing.
Question:
Answer:
Question:

70

INFORMATION GATES

Gate 8: PROJECTION

Mind Reading – Claiming to know the mind of another.
Rule #10: People are terrible mind readers.
Question: How do you know?
A good way to gain real insight into this gate is to start with some of your own projections. If you're like most people, you draw conclusions from SENSORY CUES, the way you feel around people, and from the way people look and sound when they're around you. Unless the answer to "How do you know?" is "He said so," or "She told me so," it's just mind reading.

EXAMPLES:
How do you know when someone is angry?
YOUR TURN: Answer that here.

How do you know when someone is impatient?
Answer that here.

How do you know when someone isn't listening?
Answer that here.

How do you know when someone disagrees with you?
 Answer that here.

How do you know when someone doesn't care?
Answer that here.

INSIDER'S PLAYBOOK

Now, review your answers and notice that they represent what you would be doing if you didn't care, disagreed, were impatient, etc. That's why this gate is called the gate of PROJECTION!

Go back through your answers and answer this question.

WHAT ELSE COULD THE SENSORY CUE MEAN?
Angry Sensory Cue

Impatient Sensory Cue

Not listening Sensory Cue

Disagrees Sensory Cue

Doesn't Care Sensory Cue

Whenever you hear, "He has no respect for my authority." or "You don't understand." or "She never hears a word I say!" that's your cue to ask, "How do you know?" followed by "What else could it mean?

INFORMATION GATES

Gate 9: SUPERIORITY

Life Rulers – Personal rules applied to others.

Living by your own rules is one thing. Requiring others to live by your personal rules is something else entirely

1. List your own Life Rulers here. What are the aphorisms and sayings that you've internalized and say often to the people around you? Where did you learn them?

2. For the next 24 to 48 hours, listen for Life Rulers, and write them down.

3. For the following 24 hours, find out the source of every Life Ruler you hear. Ask, "Where did you learn that?" and "According to whom?" Or "Who told you that?" Write down your results here:

INSIDER'S PLAYBOOK

USING THE 9 GATES QUESTIONS

Every (yes, every) statement contains numerous gates through which you can drive to get to the deep structure. If you open a gate that leads to a dead end, backup and try another route. To integrate these questions into your behavior, come up with 3 example statements for each gate, along with the questions that would take you deeper.

REVIEW OF THE GATES:

CONFUSION

INACTION

STUCK

INHIBITION

ABSTRACTION

BLAME

EXCUSES

PROJECTION

SUPERIORITY

74

INFORMATION GATES

REVIEW OF TAXI DRIVING RULES

Rule #1: The way to know what someone means is to ask.
This is how you avoid the dead ends and detours.

Rule #2: Blend with what you see and hear.
This helps your passenger trust you enough to let you drive

Rule #3: Backtrack before asking questions
This helps your passenger know what info you're asking for

Rule #4: There are always missing W's.
This helps you to maintain the basic conversation

Rule #5: All verbs are vague.
This helps you to understand how your passenger thinks

Rule #6: Always get the nouns before the verbs.
This helps your passenger avoid more confusion

Rule #7: Turn general into specific
This helps you to get someplace instead of anyplace

Rule #8: It's never about X. It's about the sensory cue
This helps you to pay attention to traffic signals

Rule #9: There is always a choice.
This helps you to find a way

Rule #10: People are terrible mind readers.
This helps you to resist the temptation to guess

BE THE PASSENGER

Write down one of your own limitations, and use the nine questions to open the gates and discover a deeper truth about yourself.

EXAMPLE: I'm no good at math.
Question: What kind of math are you no good at?
Answer: Algebra.
Question: How do you know that you're no good at algebra?
Answer: I just can't do it.
Question: What stops you from being able to do it?
Answer: It's too hard.
Question: What's too hard about doing algebra?
Answer: I get confused.
Question: You get confused when doing algebra?
Answer: Yes.
Question: Confused in what way?
Answer: I can't think clearly.
Question: What stops you from thinking clearly?
Answer: I get scared.
Question: Scared of what?
Answer: Not knowing the answer.
Question: So when you fear not knowing the answer, you can't think straight, and that's what stops you from doing algebra?
Answer: Yes.
Question: If you didn't get scared, do you think you'd be able to do better with algebra?
Answer: I don't know.

YOUR TURN:

13

TRANSITIONAL OPENERS

Every persuasion interaction has three phases. Phase One is trust building and information gathering. Phase two is the transition, where you complete listening, and begin the shift to your proposition using Openers. Phase three is when you present your persuasion proposition. The purpose of a transitional phase is to open the way for what you are about to say. You can use it to assure your persuadee that you have listened and understood. You can highlight what you've learned that can increase acceptance of what you will propose. And you can prepare them, as you give them a taste of where you intend to go with your proposal.

At the point of transition, you should have some insight into your persuadee's motivations, and your persuadee's likely position on your proposition. Strong, weak, or opposed.

YOUR TURN: Right now, as if you have already listened and are ready to transition, what do you know about your persuadee's motivations?

What do you know about your persuadee's likely position on your proposition? Strong, weak, or expect opposition?

INSIDER'S PLAYBOOK

HOW TO BUILD YOUR TRANSITION.

1. Review what you learned about your persuadee's MAP.
2. Use an opener
3. Direct what you way to what you've learned.

OPENERS

1. ASK FOR PERMISSION

a. Great opener with Need-Style for approval / appreciation
b. Gives persuadee something to say yes to
c. Tells your persuadee to get ready to think

Form: May I have two minutes of your time to tell you about my product/service, idea?

PRODUCT EXAMPLE: May I have five minutes to tell you about a way to improve your health and physical fitness in only ten minutes a day?

SERVICE EXAMPLE: May I have ten minutes of your time to talk with you about a very affordable new way to run your house on solar power?

IDEA EXAMPLE: May I have your attention for just a few minutes, so I can tell you about a simple system that will help you become the masterful persuader you desire to be?

YOUR TURN: Write a statement asking permission to present your persuasion proposition, in both a friendly style, and an enthusiastic style. Write it a second time, and refine it to make it friendlier or more interesting. Practice saying it out loud with caring and enthusiasm.

TRANSITIONAL OPENERS

2. CLAIM THE BRIDGE

a. Great opener, when direct and to the point, with Need-Style for action
b. Great opener, when indirect and exploratory, with Need-Style for accuracy
c. Great opener when time is short and there are other items on the agenda.

FORM: I 'm about to tell you about a product/service/ idea that will benefit you greatly.

PRODUCT EXAMPLE: I'm going to tell you about a simple and effective way to get the equivalent of a 90 minute workout's worth of muscle tone and bone strength in only ten minutes a day.

SERVICE EXAMPLE: It's time for you to rethink SOLAR. Because it is now possible to run your house on solar power without any upfront costs, permit hassles or performance worries. I'm about to tell you how to get it for yourself.

IDEA EXAMPLE: You can master the art of persuasion. Here's how.

YOUR TURN: Write a statement that declares your intention to present your persuasion proposition, in both a detailed and matter of fact way, and in a no fluff and to the point way. Write it a second time, and refine it to make it more direct and with more details. Practice saying it out loud, using unspecified language. Then practice saying it out loud in a direct and assertive way.

3. THOUGHT PROVOKING STATEMENT

a. Great opener when speaking to a group
b. Great opener to create interest where there is little to none

Whenever you open with a thought-provoking statement, give it a moment to actually provoke a thought in your persuadee. Watch and listen for the beginning of a reaction. Then as soon as you think they're thinking about it, follow it up with something substantial that easily makes a lot of sense!

FORM: Thought provoking statement. Wait for visible response. Say something substantial and understandable.

PRODUCT EXAMPLE: When it comes to how you take care of your body, are you using it or losing it? (Pause) Let me tell you about the easiest, most effective and most enjoyable piece of exercise equipment you'll ever own.

SERVICE EXAMPLE: Did you know that there is enough energy from the sun falling on the earth every day to power all of humanity's energy needs for a year? (Pause) Until now, the problem was how to capture and use it. That's all about to change.

IDEA EXAMPLE: It's not what you know; it's what you do with what you know that counts. (Pause) But it's knowing what to do that makes it possible to do anything. I'd like to tell you exactly what to do in order to turn what you now know about persuasion into action and results.

YOUR TURN: Create or find a thought provoking statement that contains words that play the key role in your persuasion proposition. Use quote books or google your keywords on the web. Then preview your persuasion proposition, using those same key words, in a way that makes sense.

TRANSITIONAL OPENERS

4. ASK FOR A YES

a. Great opener when people are inclined to agree with you
b. Great opener when someone else preceded you

You can use this opener, in a quick sequence of questions with YES as the intended result, to build a YES set. What questions related to your proposal are likely to get a YES answer from your persuadee?

FORM: Ask a question, get a yes. Ask another question, get a yes. Ask another question, get a yes. Make your pitch.

PRODUCT EXAMPLE: Do you want to protect yourself against osteoporosis and loss of balance as you age? Would you be interested in how to get 90 minutes worth of exercise in ten painless minutes a day? Let me tell you about...

SERVICE EXAMPLE: Do you ever wish that sustainable energy, like solar, was cheaper and easier to use than oil? Have you ever thought about running your home on solar energy? Because now you can be part of the solution instead of part of the problem, and it won't cost you any more than you are currently paying for energy.

IDEA EXAMPLE: Ever had an idea shot down? Ever been at a loss for words? Ever wished people would show more interest in your opinion? Let me tell you how you can increase your persuasive power, prepare yourself for the clever comeback, and gain more authority and credibility when you speak

YOUR TURN: 3 questions to get a YES response

Question 1:
Question 2:
Question 3:

INSIDER'S PLAYBOOK

5. SHORT STORY

a. Great opener to build interest
b. Great opener when respected sources support you

Stories give us the lessons of other people's experiences. Stories give us a safe place to reflect on our situation and ourselves. Testimonials are short, personal stories.

FORM: Introduce your proposal with a story/testimonial.

PRODUCT EXAMPLE: I wish there were 48 hours in a day, because I have so much to do. So when my wife promised to show me a proven way to get an hour and a half of exercise in ten minutes, I was interested. She took me to a new shop in town, where a smiling woman on a machine appeared to be jiggling her from head to toe. A beep and the movement stopped. "I love that!" she declared to no one in particular. I had to try it. Now I have one of my own.

SERVICE EXAMPLE: Everyone knows the downside of our dependence on foreign oil, and the danger of climate change. Well, according to Ed B, you can do something about both things that costs nothing up front, and saves you money in the long run.

IDEA EXAMPLE: I just heard from an M.D. who has been doing the activities in the Playbook. Here's what he wrote: "Rick, I can see why some of my efforts with persuasion have been so not successful. I just finished with a new patient. What a difference it makes to be able to motivate people to own the desire to change. I really appreciate your book!" I think you'll appreciate it too!

YOUR TURN: What's a short story you could tell to introduce your persuasion proposition? Where can you get a testimonial story that you can use to introduce your persuasion proposition?

TRANSITIONAL OPENERS

6. RELEVANT QUOTE OR APHORISM

a. Great opener to build credibility
b. Great opener to get interest right out of the gate

"If you would persuade, you must appeal to interest rather than intellect." Quotes and aphorisms add authority to your words. Even an anonymous quote grants some authority. An aphorism is a brief expression of an important principle that you seek to employ, through the clever turn of a phrase, pun, or paradox.

PRODUCT EXAMPLE: It has been said that the time you don't find for exercise is the time that finds you for illness.

SERVICE EXAMPLE: Some people believe that we'll only have solar power when utility companies figure out how to run a beam of sunlight through a meter.

IDEA EXAMPLE: You've heard the saying, 'Think outside of the box.' Here's my version. "Don't get in the box!" This Playbook will help you stay out of the box, and help you get other people out of them too!

YOUR TURN: What's an aphorism or relevant quote that naturally leads in the direction of your persuasion proposition?

7. HOPEFUL OR TERRIFYING COMPARISON

a. Great opener when people are complacent
b. Great opener when people are afraid

A hopeful comparison says things can turn out better, as compared to how bad they are now, if your persuadee takes your desired action. A terrifying comparison says that things may well turn out worse, compared to how good they are now, unless your persuadee takes your desired action.

FORM: Define the best case or worst-case scenario, and connect it to your persuasion proposition. In both cases, end the comparison with the point you seek to highlight.

PRODUCT EXAMPLE: If you fail to exercise, the loss of bone mass and muscle tone as you age will make the simplest things harder to do. Here's how to find the time now.

SERVICE EXAMPLE: What will the world be like for our children's children if we keep throwing carbon into our atmosphere and driving climate change? What if there was a way to use sustainable sources of energy that didn't destroy our environment? There is. It's here now. And it will save you money, too.

IDEA EXAMPLE: Just think of the money you may have lost, the opportunity you may have missed, and your best ideas that didn't get needed support because of a failure to persuade. Compare that to being in the right place, at the right time, with the right approach to get the right things to happen! The difference? The Playbook.

YOUR TURN: What's the worst-case scenario of not implementing your proposition? What's the best-case scenario if it is implemented? Take it to extremes, and then back up a little until you find it credible and compelling.

TRANSITIONAL OPENERS

8. HISTORICAL PERSPECTIVE

a. Great opener to provide context for your proposition
b. Great opener to highlight progress
c. Great opener to demonstrate a successful or failed solution

FORM: Use 'then and now,' or 'Let's take a look back at what brought us to this moment in time,' or 'Let's look ahead at where we'll be if we make some changes now.

PRODUCT EXAMPLE: Is it important to you to have healthy bones and joints in the later years of your life? How about strength and muscle tone? How will you get there? Let me tell you about an amazing piece of equipment that only takes ten minutes a day…

SERVICE EXAMPLE: For the past ten years, we've known that energy related pollution is driving climate change. Twenty years from now, unless we change course, we will have hell to pay. So let me tell you about a revolutionary service that can help us change that now.

IDEA EXAMPLE: Consider what you knew about persuasion when you first reading through the Playbook. Now imagine what you will be able to accomplish when you have completed it. Today's skills will be there for you tomorrow.

YOUR TURN: What in the past gave your persuasion proposition a reason to be in the present? What future will result if your persuadee accepts your proposition? How can you draw a line connecting the past, and the choice, to that future right now?

REVIEW OF TRANSITIONAL OPENERS

- **ASK FOR PERMISSION.**
- **CLAIM THE BRIDGE.**
- **THOUGHT PROVOKING STATEMENT.**
- **ASK FOR A YES.**
- **SHORT STORY OR TESTIMONIAL.**
- **RELEVANT QUOTE OR APHORISM**
- **HOPEFUL OR TERRIFYING COMPARISON**
- **HISTORICAL PERSPECTIVE**

14

ORGANIZING THEMES

If you organize your persuasion proposition around a theme, that theme becomes the backbone that helps your persuadee keep track of where you were, where you are, and where you're going. Themes typically have an opening, a body, and a close. The body of a theme can be as long or as short as the time available.

For example, a speech is a persuasion proposition lasting an hour to two hours. A training program is a persuasion proposition lasting several hours. A sales pitch for a vibrational exerciser might take ten to fifteen minutes. The longer the body of your presentation, the more key ideas can be conveyed, up to a point.

The conscious mind can pay attention to 7 plus or minus 2 chunks of information. So the maximum number of key ideas in a long training program is 9. How many? 9. Each of these key ideas can have 7 plus or minus 2 key points. But people are cognitive misers. So fewer is usually better.

Also, the less time you have, the fewer key ideas to convey. In fact, 3 big ideas are plenty for a half hour to an hour of persuasion time (a speech).

INSIDER'S PLAYBOOK

In this section of the Playbook, use the openers you developed in the previous section to get your persuasion juices flowing.

Your goal in this chapter: Develop an outline for the body of your proposition using one of the following themes.

In the examples that follow, I'm assuming a five to ten minute pitch, and will outline accordingly. I'm limiting myself to one of my three example propositions for each theme.

1. THE TIMELINE
a. Great theme when you opened with historical perspective.
b. Great theme when you want your proposition perceived as part of or a break from an established direction.

PRODUCT EXAMPLE OUTLINE
1. PAST: What is the origin of this type of equipment?
Russian Cosmonauts, as a way to deal with bone density.
Then athletes started using it. Professional football teams. Pro bicyclists. Pro Golfers. Use in a medical clinic over a three-year trial. Results. Testimonials.
2. PRESENT: Who is using it now? What are they learning? How is it used?
    NASA
    Current research
    My own experience with V.E.

3. FUTURE: What can you expect when you start using V.E. as part of your daily routine?
    How to us the exerciser
    How to maximize the benefits

YOUR TURN:

ORGANIZING THEMES

PROBLEM AND SOLUTION

a. Great theme to reveal the depth of a problem, the consequences of a problem, and tie your solution to the end of the problem. Make sure the emphasis of what you say is on the solution.

SERVICE EXAMPLE OUTLINE:
Two problems:
>Our addiction to oil.
>The cost of breaking the addiction.

The consequence:
>A great deal of money in the hands of people who hate us
>The world's weather systems are becoming increasingly unpredictable.
>Poor adoption of solar has meant the cost still stays way out of reach for the vast majority of people

The solution:
>Solar energy marketed as a service
>The company designs your solar system.
>The company installs the equipment and loans it to you (Like the phone company does with telephone wires)
>You pay for your energy, even though your house is now generating it. The company gets paid and is profitable.

YOUR TURN:

INSIDER'S PLAYBOOK

3. MEETING THE CHALLENGE

a. Great theme to take a difficult situation based in fact and convert it to an emotionally powerful cause.
b. Great theme when people are frightened by the problem

IDEA EXAMPLE OUTLINE:

The Challenge: Learning requires thought, and thinking is hard work. That's why it's much easier to start something than it is to finish it. Here you have a long book filled with exercises and activities. Just the thought of it makes it seem like a difficult task. Why do it?

Because, if not you, then who? Who else will change your world for the better if not you? And if not now, when? You are always busy. And all sorts of things happen and events intrude. To succeed at what you set out to do when you first picked up the Playbook, you must summon just a small amount of will and self determination, just enough to take another step forward. The journey is long, but it begins with a single step. I'll tell you what to do and how to do it. The results are almost certainly achievable. The only question is, do you intend to achieve them! Because the only way you can fail is if you fail to step up and finish what you've begun. The choice to succeed or fail is yours. But there is no question that you do have this chance to find out what you're made of, this chance to shape your own destiny.

YOUR TURN: What is the challenge you want to place before your persuadee? How can adopting your proposal give them something at which to succeed, or can meeting the challenge help them to avoid failure?

ORGANIZING THEMES

4. OPPORTUNITY

a. Great theme for targeting the motivation of reward.
b. Great theme to reveal what may be lost by the failure to seize this opportunity.

IDEA EXAMPLE OUTLINE:

What do you gain by finishing what you started and doing all the exercises and activities in the Playbook? The opportunities are endless

You'll discover that you can count on yourself, something you won't have to question ever again as a result of following through on this one.

The skills you found interesting at the beginning will be yours at the end. Yours!

Your influence will grow, and your world will change around you.

The opportunity in this Playbook lives in the design of it. It works best for you when you do only one chapter and one activity at a time. Since it is designed to work this way, all you have to do is take the next step rather than a whole series of steps in order to get to the end and achieve the mission of using your influence to bring about positive change in your world.

YOUR TURN: What is the opportunity for your persuadee in your persuasion proposition?

5. FEATURES AND BENEFITS

a. Ideal theme for product/service introduction/promotion.

Features speak to the logical mind. Features speak to practical decisions made for practical reasons. Benefits appeal to emotion. Benefits tell people why they should care, what's in it for them. Benefits generally speak more persuasively than features to the undecided. Present the features of your idea, product or service, and then connect those features to specific benefits that your persuadee will want to receive by making a favorable decision.

When someone already supports your proposition, an emphasis on features may prove more beneficial than an emphasis on benefits.

PRODUCT EXAMPLE OUTLINE:

Feature: It only takes 10 minutes a day to get the muscle tone equivalent of an hour and a half work out.
Benefits: What this means to you is that you have less of an excuse and more of a reason to take care of yourself, or more time for other activities because you know that you're taking care of the bottom line.
Feature: Research indicates that full body vibration helps with bone density, balance and muscle tone.
Benefits: What this means to you that your ten minutes a day will be rewarded with results.

YOUR TURN

ORGANIZING THEMES

6. MAKE AN EXAMPLE
a. Great theme to put a human face on details.

Real or fictional, let your examples reveal the need for your proposal, or demonstrate what can happen when your proposal is adopted. Let the people in your example show by their example and tell by their experience what you want your persuadee to know in making a decision.

SERVICE EXAMPLE OUTLINE:

I looked into using solar power for my home a few years ago. I hated what I was reading and hearing about climate change. I'm a frequent flyer, and I've been in several so-called 'storms of the century.' The frequency and intensity of these 'freak' weather events is definitely getting worse. So climate change is real enough to me. But the cost of solar was prohibitive, anywhere from $20K to $40K. It seemed like such a hassle. I'd have to get special permits, and meet certain city requirements. It seemed like something else to worry about, too. If something went wrong, I'd be stuck with fixing it. If the technology improved, I'd be stuck with an expensive and outdated model. My reaction? Forget about it.

But then I heard of this revolutionary way of bringing solar power to the people. It took me 6 minutes to make the decision to do it. I mean, why not? It solves every problem I ran into the last time I looked into solar power for my home.

YOUR TURN:

7. ANSWER THE QUESTIONS

a. Great theme when you want to get to know the interests and needs, motivations and positions, of your audience
b. Great theme when you are dealing with skeptics and doubters
c. Great theme for preparing people for a later presentation

Three ways to use this theme
1. Anticipate questions, ask them and answer them.
   If you don't have the opportunity to ask your persuadee, then ask yourself, what about my proposal is most likely to raise doubt, fear and uncertainty? What will those doubts be? What is there to fear? What is the cause of uncertainty? Organize what you have to say around these questions, and answer them persuasively.
2. Ask for questions, write them down, and answer them one at a time
3. Ask for questions, write them down, and organize what you have to say to answer them all at once.

When receiving questions, write them down where everyone can see them, or at least where everyone can see you writing them down. Visibly check them off as you answer them.

SERVICE EXAMPLE OUTLINE:
You may be wondering about the costs of this solar system. There are no system costs. No installation fees. No money changes hands until you approve the design. Then, you pay a $500 deposit. That money goes into an interest bearing account. At the end of your contract, it is returned to you with the interest. If others sign up as a result of you telling them, the company reduces your rate by 5% per person. Tell enough people; your cost can be absolutely nothing.

YOUR TURN:

ORGANIZING THEMES

8. INOCCULATION

Great theme when you are certain to face opposition in a group environment containing undecideds. Instead of playing defense by waiting for accusations and then trying to explain yourself, you can go on the offense, organize what you have to say by putting the frame around your opposition that best serves your needs, and addressing it accordingly. Tell your audience what your opposition may tell them, and what you want them to hear when that happens.

SERVICE EXAMPLE OUTLINE:

Now some may tell you that solar power isn't ready for prime time, that the technology isn't ready for wide adoption. Whenever you hear that, ask yourself who stands to gain from you believing it? Remind yourself that they are wrong, it is ready now, and wide adoption has to start somewhere. That's the power that you have to bring about a revolution in how we as a society power our energy needs.

Some will tell you that if it sounds too good to be true, it is too good to be true. When you hear that, I want you to remember three things. First, it is true. Second, it's really good. And third, people said the same thing about air travel and personal computers, and every other advance or breakthrough.

YOUR TURN:

9. MODEL
a. Great theme to boil something complex down into a simple idea that is memorable and learnable.

Models don't have to be true, but they do have to work. Models create order out of chaos. Whenever you hear about four ways to this, and five reasons for that, you're hearing a model of reality, not reality itself.

IDEA EXAMPLE OUTLINE:

To help you learn the art of persuasion, think of this Playbook in terms of a countdown to persuasive power. You've learned or will learn:
Ten Organizing Themes
Nine Information Gates,
Eight Openers, Themes and Guides
Seven Persuasion Signals
Six Towards and Away Motivations
Five Stages of Change
Four Possible Outcomes, and Four Need-Styles
Three Receiving Zones and Three Phases of Persuasion,
Two Ways People Listen
One Basic Belief on which everything depends.

YOUR TURN:
What model can you use to organize your persuasion proposition for maximum impact?

ORGANIZING THEMES

10. COMPONENTS

a. Great theme when you have more than one idea, product or service to introduce to your persuadee. You can use different themes for each component of your proposition, as a way of differentiating them. You might use a timeline theme to develop your proposition, and then switch to a model theme to present it. You might begin with a features benefit theme, then go to an Answer the Questions theme, and finish with a model. Or you might start with the Inoculation theme and end with a Story.

The big challenge is creating your transitions from one component to the next. In your preparation for using the components theme, identify what seems to you to be the most engaging and interesting order. Then find something in each component that you can use as leverage to introduce the next component. At the end of your presentation, assemble all the components together with a review.

YOUR TURN:
Review the work you did in this chapter. Which themes helped you deliver your persuasion proposition with the most power or cohesiveness? Pull those parts out, and sequence them below into a component theme.

INSIDER'S PLAYBOOK

REVIEW OF ORGANIZING THEMES

TIMELINE

PROBLEM AND SOLUTION

MEETING THE CHALLENGE

OPPORTUNITY

FEATURES AND BENEFITS

ANSWER THE QUESTIONS

MAKE AN EXAMPLE

INNOCULATION

MODEL

COMPONENT

15

DELIVERY GUIDES

Practice these eight delivery guides to help you take your persuasion proposition to the next level.

The KISS principle: KEEP IT SHORT AND SIMPLE!

You can do more with less.

PRODUCT EXAMPLE: 90 minutes of muscle toning in ten minutes a day.

SERVICE EXAMPLE: No system costs. No installation charges. No permit hassles. No maintenance expense. No performance worries. No rate increases.

IDEA EXAMPLE: It's not just what you know. It's what you can do with what you know. If you want your actions to speak louder than your words, you must complete the program.

YOUR TURN:

TWO PART CONTRAST

Create some psychological traction with a future that beckons, and some psychological repulsion to the status quo with a future that frightens. The result is momentum for change.

PRODUCT EXAMPLE: Which do you prefer? Fit? Or fat? Strong or brittle? Balanced or unbalanced? Ten minutes of easy exercise or 90 minutes of hard exercise?

SERVICE EXAMPLE: What does our future hold? Sustainable energy and a livable environment? Or climate crisis and terrorism? Unlimited power going into the grid, or limited power going through the grid? All the energy you need to maintain your desired lifestyle? Or brownouts, blackouts and power outages resetting your clocks?

IDEA EXAMPLE: You could read it once, and then try to remember it when you need it. Good luck with that. Or work with the material by working through the Playbook, and it becomes part of the way you think about persuasion.

YOUR TURN:

DELIVERY GUIDES

THE RULE OF THREES

Threes help us to remember details. Threes strengthen concepts. Threes turn information into formulas. Threes let you set up an expectation, confirm the expectation, and then fulfill it. It takes two points to make a line. Lines have direction. Direction sets up an expectation. Fulfillment of expectation makes something memorable.

FORM: Make your point. Confirm it with another point of the same type. Then drop in the third point of the same type.

PRODUCT EXAMPLE: You know you need to exercise. You know the value of your time. And you know that if you knew there was a way to attend to both, you'd know it must be time.

SERVICE EXAMPLE: Powering your home with Solar Power is Possible. Powering your home with Solar Power is Responsible. And if you want to Power your home with Solar Power, it's available now at a completely affordable price.

IDEA EXAMPLE: First you learn how to count. Then you learn how to add and subtract. Then you learned how to multiply and divide. Learning the art of persuasion works exactly the same way.

YOUR TURN:

INSIDER'S PLAYBOOK

RHETORICAL QUESTIONS

When people hear a question followed by an answer, they find the answer more believable and compelling than a statement of fact. If you limit your use of this guide, and stay open to feedback, then rhetorical questions add a powerful tool to your persuasion toolbox. Combine this with other guides for maximum effect.

FORM: Ask the question to raise the point. Answer the question to make the point.

PRODUCT EXAMPLE: If you're wondering how it feels to do vibrational exercise, it feels wonderful.

SERVICE EXAMPLE: If the design is right, is it really possible to power my home and lifestyle with solar energy? Yes, the result is predictable and measurable. Will it work as well as what you have now? It will work much better, because you'll still be connected to the grid. Now, could it become more expensive in the future? No! Your rate is locked in when you sign up to have your home evaluated for the service.

IDEA EXAMPLE: Do you really need to complete the Playbook for it to be useful? No, some people find it beneficial right from the outset. Use it like a Playbook. Got a problem? Need a solution? Pick a play and go for it. Would it be worth it to do all the activities in the entire Playbook? You bet. The more you learn, the more you understand. The more you understand, the greater your confidence. If confidence is what you need to be more persuasive, then you know what you need to do. Learn the Playbook!

YOUR TURN:

DELIVERY GUIDES

REPEAT AND RESTATER, restate and repeat.

Some say it takes seven exposures to an idea before it takes hold. That's where you tell someone that you're going to tell them something shortly, but then you don't tell them. Then you tell them you're about to tell them. But you hold off on telling them. Each telling builds response potential.

Repetition increases comprehension and deepens consideration of your idea. A little repetition leads to a lot of persuasion, but too much repetition leads to frustration and aggravation.

FORM: Say something. Say it again in a different way. Then say it again, only differently.

PRODUCT EXAMPLE: My wife and I enjoy the Jiggler. We take turns. We use jiggling as hang out time, or a chance to talk during our busy days. She enjoys it when I jiggle as much as when she jiggles. I feel the same way. I promise you this: The family that jiggles together giggles together.

SERVICE EXAMPLE: If you care about energy independence, if you want your country to be free of dependence on the oil economy, if you want to use sustainable energy that puts energy into the grid, then you owe it to yourself to look into the only energy business that offers energy independence to its subscribers.

IDEA EXAMPLE: Keep going. Keep going. Keep going. Learn the Playbook. Learn the rules. Learn the plays.

YOUR TURN:

MAKE YOUR POINT OBVIOUS

If there is a point you're trying to make, either make the point first and then illustrate it, or make the point last and make it really obvious.

FORM: The bottom line about the product, service or idea in the fewest number of words.

PRODUCT EXAMPLE: Vibrational Exercise has proven benefits for your health and well-being.

SERVICE EXAMPLE: There is now every reason to say yes to solar power for your home

IDEA EXAMPLE: You don't really understand any of it until you understand all of it.

YOUR TURN:

DELIVERY GUIDES

BE DIRECTIVE

Give people a direction. Ask for an outcome. Ask for what you want. An undirected mind tends to fixate on what it doesn't want. Tell them where you're going to take them, or tell them what you'd like to have happen, and they can simply follow you to get there. The more specific you are about a direction, the more likely it is that things will move in that direction. Direction persuades, particularly when it is the only real alternative to fight or flight.

FORM: During your presentation, ask directly for what you want.

PRODUCT EXAMPLE: Interested? Then contact my wife for more information.

SOLAR EXAMPLE: If you do nothing else, please watch the video at the website.

IDEA EXAMPLE: Keep going, step by step, until you have finished the Playbook.

YOUR TURN:

INSIDER'S PLAYBOOK

USE VIVID LANGUAGE

While statistics have some appeal to the logical listener, emotional listeners tend to tune them out or get lost in them. Examples make them vivid enough to understand and remember. Statistics fail to deliver a persuasive message, in part, because of the low opinion most people have of them. Examples are easier to comprehend and understand than statistics

FORM: Give your numbers if you must. Then illustrate with an example. An isolated example. An example of the desirable generalization. Or offer a counter example.

PRODUCT EXAMPLE: Studies showed a significant improvement in circulation. All I know is, I walk in. Step up. Start the cycle. Ten minutes later, it beeps and stops. And I feel awake, alert and enthusiastic. I feel fantastic.

SERVICE EXAMPLE: There are only 14000 active solar homes in the United States. That's no way to start a revolution. There should be millions. You ought to have it. Your neighbors ought to have it. Your entire community ought to have it. It takes someone like you to get the ball rolling. Someone has to be number 14,001.

IDEA EXAMPLE: Studies show that your odds of finishing a how-to book are a little less than %50. I know a guy who missed a promotion just a month ago, because he didn't know how to speak persuasively, and the other guy clearly did.

YOUR TURN:

DELIVERY GUIDES

RULES FOR THE USE OF NUMBERS:

1. Statistics should support your point, not the reverse. When developing your persuasion proposition, start with your points and then find supporting data

PRODUCT EXAMPLE: The point is, it's good for you. The statistics prove it.

SERVICE EXAMPLE: The point is, it will save you money. The statistics demonstrate it.

IDEA EXAMPLE: The point is, your learning will last longer. Statistics reveal retention rates.

YOUR TURN:

2. Sometimes it is better to round off, sometimes it's not. Usually it is. But not in science, engineering, or any time precision is essential ore required

3. Make big numbers personal.

PRODUCT EXAMPLE: What are spending on insurance every month? What do you get back for it? Now consider the cost of the Jiggler, and what you'll get back for it.

SERVICE EXAMPLE: How will you explain to your grandchildren the failure of this generation to be responsible stewards of our resources?

IDEA EXAMPLE: In the face of ignorance, at what point does having knowledge become an unfair advantage?

YOUR TURN:

4. Turn numbers into ideas.

PRODUCT EXAMPLE: How big is it? It has a smaller footprint than an exercise bike, by about half.

SERVICE EXAMPLE: How fast can this catch on? You only need a few hundred people a month across the entire country to sign up for this service, and you'll have 20% of the country on solar power in fifteen years.

IDEA EXAMPLE: It isn't the number of chapters, pages, and points that matters. It's working with the material so that you have experience with it that counts!

5. Turn numbers into pictures

The nice thing about a picture is that you can show it to people while you talk. Since a picture is worth a thousand words, this adds power to what you are saying.

PRODUCT EXAMPLE: Bone density before and after using the Jiggler.

SERVICE EXAMPLE: Amount of atmospheric carbon reduced by the use of solar energy

IDEA EXAMPLE: Success rates of certified change artists compared to casual readers.

YOUR TURN:

6. Many numbers? Use a handout, not a conversation.

7. Brief bulleted and numbered lists work

They help people to make sense out of numbers, and to remember points, by predigesting and organizing them into a sequence.

16

FUNNY PERSUASION

Humor breaks down the barriers that keep us divided and polarized.

Humor builds bridges to bring us together.

Humor attracts interest, puts people on common footing, and creates an atmosphere of goodwill that is conducive to meaningful communication.

Humor discharges resistance, overcomes stubbornness, and creates opportunity for dialog.

Humor is persuasive.

It's not hard to be funny, but it does take a willingness to risk. One of the most difficult jobs in the world is making people laugh, IF you tell them you're going to. Humor is risky enough without making it harder than it needs to be! Don't say something is funny. Say something funny!!!

NONVERBAL EXAGGERATION CAN BE FUNNY
(If you could see me now, you'd be cracking up)

Nonverbal humor makes verbal humor funnier. Verbal humor, without nonverbal humor to support it, can be risky business. A facial expression, a playful voice tone, an exaggerated gesture all help in making persuasion fun, and yes, funny. If it is appropriate, how can you use non-verbal communication to exaggerate or have fun while presenting your persuasion proposition?

PRODUCT EXAMPLE: Go through the motions of lifting weights, and make a face about how unpleasant it is. Then pretend to be jiggling, and look very happy and satisfied!

SERVICE EXAMPLE: When talking about terrorists, pretend to be holding a newspaper, shake my head 'NO' in disgust.

IDEA EXAMPLE: If you could see me, I'm doing it now. I'm looking at you as if doing this particular activity is the most exciting thing in your world, and wanting you to nod your head in agreement. Right? Right? Ok, go ahead.

YOUR TURN: (See?)

FUNNY PERSUASION

UNPLEASANT SURPRISES CAN BE FUNNY
(Oops. Ouch. Whoa. What? Dang!)

If you make a mistake, or flub a word in front of an audience, make fun of yourself and your persuadee may laugh.

PRODUCT EXAMPLE: Call the Vibrational Exerciser a VIBRATOR, then look embarrassed, and say Vibrational sexerciser, then shake it off, and say, Jiggler. (This actually happened to me once! Now I do it on purpose just to have fun talking about the V.E.)

SERVICE EXAMPLE: The first time I use the term 'Solar System,' I can look surprised at the double meaning, and then wonder aloud about how you, like me, may be wondering how we're going to get all the planets and moons up on the roof, and if the new design will include Pluto, now downgraded from a planet to a large rock!

IDEA EXAMPLE: People say the strangest things when you practice the art of persuasion in public. Back when I was young and stupid, I was called in to make a proposal to a local business; I purposefully tried to have fun with it. When I was done, the HR guy who brought me in patted on the back and, loud enough for everyone in the room to hear he said, "You killed em!" People say the strangest things to wish you well. It turns out that 'you killed the audience' is actually a good thing to be told, just like 'break a leg,' or 'knock em' dead,' is a nice thing to hear from another performer. But when I heard "You killed em'," I felt terrible about it. I said 'Tell me what I did wrong!' and the room behind us erupted in laughter. The joke, as they say, was on me!

YOUR TURN: How could surprise either yourself or your persuadee while making your presentation? (Yes, it's okay if it's contrived. It may not be new to you, but it will be new to your persuadee!)

INSIDER'S PLAYBOOK

A PLAY ON WORDS CAN BE FUNNY
(Time flies like an arrow. Fruit flies like banana.)

There are all kinds of ways to play with words, including accents, puns, malapropisms, mispronunciations, or calling something by the wrong name. Phrases can be funny. Ridicule can be funny. Being serious about funny things or being funny about serious things can be funny.

PRODUCT EXAMPLE: The Jiggler. No fat cell left behind. And no fat cells left in my behind.

SERVICE EXAMPLE: Solar Power. Finally, a bright idea! I heard about it and a lightbulb went off in my head! When it came back on, it was sustainable.

IDEA EXAMPLE: The Playbook: Where your words are mightier than my pen! When others are playing by the book, it's a better book to play by!

YOUR TURN:

TIMING MAKES FUNNY
(Wait for it...wait for it...)
Timing is everything. Time of day. Time in the meeting. A difficult time in a person's life. Read your persuadee carefully, and make sure that the time is right for something fun or funny.

FUNNY PERSUASION

BAD DELIVERY CAN BE FUNNY
(If you, um, don't, er, well, I, never mind.)

Perhaps the funniest thing of all is when someone butchers a joke.

PRODUCT EXAMPLE: That reminds me of a joke. There was a guy on his way to the gym. No wait, he hated going to the gym. Yeah, there was this guy who hated going to the gym. But he couldn't find a way to get out of it. Um, a way to wiggle out of it. Wait. He didn't have to wiggle out of it, because he could jiggle out of it. Never mind. The point is, jiggling beats going to the gym.

SERVICE EXAMPLE: When I told my 5 year old niece about solar energy for our home, she asked if it works the same way you use a magnifying glass to get the sun to burn leaves. I told her, no, honey, if you had a magnifying glass big enough to do that to your house, it would be called a DEATHRAY!

IDEA EXAMPLE: The Praybook. er...I mean Playbook. It's the Insider's Guide To The Art Of Perspiration.

YOUR TURN:

INSIDER'S PLAYBOOK

IRONY CAN BE FUNNY
(Funnier than an irony deficiency!)

When you say one thing but mean something else, and your tone betrays your actual meaning, that's ironic humor. Overstating the case (hyperbole,) or understating the case (hypobole?) can also be ironically funny. But the best use of ironic humor? Find a paradox and expose it.

PRODUCT EXAMPLE: Vibrational exercise gives people who hate exercise an unfair advantage!

SERVICE EXAMPLE: Ironically, we're going to have solar energy one way or another. You can either heat your house with it to stay warm in the winter, or you can heat the planet it with it and be warm all year long.

IDEA EXAMPLE: Ironically, I'm trying to persuade you to learn to be persuasive by persuading you to do what you are already doing. Dang, I'm good!

YOUR TURN:

FUNNY PERSUASION

HUMOR IS UNRULY. HERE ARE THE RULES.

Funny Rule #1: FIND YOUR OWN FUNNY

You know what's funny? Yes, you do. Watch for it. Listen for it. Appreciate it when it happens. Most people say funny things once in a while, and quite often by accident. Ask yourself, why am I laughing? Chances are, if it makes you laugh, you can use it to make others laugh.

PRODUCT EXAMPLE: I discovered that if I look at myself in a mirror while engaged in vibrational exercise, I can see every part of my body jiggle! Trust me, once you've seen yourself jiggle, it's easy to understand the meaning of the word. It's like your wiggle is dancing a little jig. It's even funnier if you're wearing a wig. If I sell you a Jiggler, then Jigglers are my gig!

SERVICE EXAMPLE: You know what's funny? Solar power is a lot like nuclear power; only the nuclear plant is safely away from the planet! You know what else is funny? How much energy people will expend to defend doing nothing versus doing the intelligent thing and switching their home to solar power.

IDEA EXAMPLE: You know what's funny? The Playbook can make you more persuasive. But it can't make you any smarter. So there's still a way to screw this up. That's with your own 'better idea.'

YOUR TURN: What's funny about your persuasion proposition? If nothing, what can make it funny? How would a funny person deliver it?

INSIDER'S PLAYBOOK

Funny Rule #2: POINT TO A POINT

This rule is a 2 parter. First, have a point. Second, stay on message. This is easier than it sounds. All you have to do is tie your funny to your proposition, using JUNK O'LOGIC. This is an Irish concept apparently, like FILET O'FISH. Actually, it's an advertising concept, where you talk like two unrelated ideas are related. In this case, your attempt at humor and your proposition. So even if your funny and your point aren't actually related, they become related the moment you say they are.

PRODUCT EXAMPLE: And the bartender said, "That's not my dog." And you know, when it comes to finding an hour and a half to exercise every day, that's not my dog, either.

SERVICE EXAMPLE: And the string said, "I'm a frayed knot." But when it comes to switching to solar power for my home, I'm not afraid. But I am tired of being strung along like an oil addict from utility bill to utility bill.

IDEA EXAMPLE: My wife is so immature. Whenever I'm in the bathtub, she comes in and sinks my ducks! But the only thing that can sink your persuasion efforts is a lack of preparation. Think of the Playbook as a relaxing bath that you can take before going out on a persuasion date.

YOUR TURN:

FUNNY PERSUASION

Funny Rule #3: SHORT IS FUNNIER THAN LONG

Think of funny as punctuation rather than paragraphs. Quick one-liners and the occasional play on word are usually funnier persuaders than long stories that have no point.

Funny Rule #4: TIMING

Put your funny to the test. Try it out on a few people, notice their reaction, work on your timing. Good timing means waiting long enough for people to get the joke. After your punch line, say these words to yourself. "Wait for it. Wait for it." After a moment, if you haven't gotten a response, say to yourself, 'Stop waiting. Stop waiting." And then next time, remember to punch up your punch line NON VERBALLY so it is obviously there!

Funny Rule #4: NEVER TELEGRAPH PUNCHES

Never say that you're going to say something funny. That way, if it turns out that it's not that funny, nobody will be the wiser.

In conclusion, let me point out that there are three kinds of people in the world. Those who can count, and those who can't. Moving on.

17

SEVEN SIGNALS INTRODUCTION

People try to avoid having to think whenever and wherever possible. In part, this is because thinking for oneself is not encouraged in much of the world. In part, it's because there is so much going on that it's difficult to keep up! Easier to generalize, delete, distort and otherwise convert new information into old and familiar information. Instead of paying attention and questioning what we see and hear, people in strong feeling states like tired, overwhelmed or stressed, tend to look and listen for shortcuts and signals about the meaning and worth of ideas, products and services rather than having to think about them.

When a person listens logically, they are interested in facts, details, and other high quality information that they can use to evaluate what you are saying. But unless a person has grown up with a lot of support for critical thinking, you can expect to be talking to someone who is listening emotionally a good deal of the time. It just isn't enough to have the facts on your side. You've got to be able to speak to people who are barely thinking! By adding one or more of the seven Persuasion Signals from the next seven chapters, you increase the persuasive power of your proposition.

18

THE SIGNAL OF AFFINITY

PEOPLE LIKE PEOPLE WHO ARE LIKE THEM

If they share your background, or have work in common with you, or you have mutual friends, or agree about anything that you value, they resonate familiarity and approachability.

PRODUCT EXAMPLE: Find areas of similarity. Age. Weight. Health history. Health concerns. Current exercise regime.

SERVICE EXAMPLE: Save money. Protect the environment. Concern for the future. Concern for the children.

IDEA EXAMPLE: Desire to have more influence. Interest in understanding what makes people tick. Interest in learning. Curiosity about how things work.

YOUR TURN: In what way are you like your persuadee? In what way is your proposition familiar for your persuadee?

INSIDER'S PLAYBOOK

PEOPLE LIKE PEOPLE THEY WANT TO BE LIKE

People like attractive people. What makes people attractive? Popularity. Charm. The way you put yourself together. The rule in professional speaking is to always dress a little nicer than the audience. The rule in product persuasion is have an attractive presentation. People like admirable people. What makes people admirable? Your self-control. The way you carry yourself. The way you respond to questions and requests. In promoting a product, talk with confidence. In promoting a service, deliver it in an admirable way. If an idea, much of the material in this program makes it more admirable and attractive.

PRODUCT EXAMPLE: Fresh paper towels to stand on during public presentations. Smile and greeting. No clutter around the Jiggler. Set an example by going first.

SERVICE EXAMPLE: Attractive colors on your literature. Attractive or popular spokespeople. Appeal to highest ideals and basic values.

IDEA EXAMPLE: Speak from a little father down the road. "I was once where you are. I learned this. Now you can join me here."

YOUR TURN: How can you make yourself and/or your proposition more attractive to your persuadee? What aspect of you or your proposition is admirable?

THE SIGNAL OF AFFINITY

PEOPLE LIKE PEOPLE WHO LIKE THEM

People know you like them when you build them up instead of tearing them down, when you give praise and compliments rather than criticism and condemnation. You can always find a reason to give an honest compliment or authentic appreciation, even if it's nothing more than "Thanks for being so honest about how you feel."

PEOPLE LIKE RESPECTFUL PEOPLE

Seek to understand. Be willing to hear an opposing view. Consider your persuadee's needs and interest as important as you consider your own.

PEOPLE LIKE WHAT PEOPLE THEY LIKE, LIKE

If someone your persuadee likes recommends you or your product, their liking of that someone makes them more inclined to like you too! Get other people who like you, your product, your service or your idea to give testimonials about you, the product, the service, or other ideas of yours, and create positive associations between your proposal and your persuadee's favorite projects, people and ideas.

YOUR TURN: Who do you know that your persuadee either knows or knows of and respects, who might be easier to persuade than your persuadee?

INSIDER'S PLAYBOOK

HOW TO PROTECT YOURSELF

These thoughts could be warning signs: "What a coincidence!" "Gosh, you're just like me!" "We agree about everything!"

Keyword: GULLIBLE

When someone tries to take advantage of your affinity with him or her, here's how to protect yourself from possible bad intent. It's easy! Just think for yourself! Notice what is being asked of you, and separate it in your mind from the person asking it.

PRODUCT EXAMPLE: Dr. Rick's a great guy. But what do I think about vibrational exercise? Is this good for me?

SERVICE EXAMPLE: Dr. Rick's a good person. He obviously cares about the future of our world. But is this service right for me? Does it work for me based on its own merit?

IDEA EXAMPLE: Yes, Dr. Rick is a fun person to learn from. And he's obviously put a lot of time, energy and thought into building this Playbook. But am I really deepening my learning by doing these exercises? How much would I remember if I wasn't doing them?

19

THE SIGNAL OF COMPARISON

It's not about liking. It's about comparison.

Comparison: To consider one thing in the light of another. Start with a benchmark to stabilize the judgment of the person you want to persuade for better or worse. Then introduce another element and make the comparison.

Not all comparisons are persuasive. Compare one person's performance to another person's performance, and the person who comes up the lesser is likely to get defensive. Tell your poorly behaved child how they measure up next to their well-behaved child, and the sibling rivalry you initiate may last a lifetime. Unless, of course, the lesser child compares such parenting to some positive parenting they see on the teevee. Then the child can dismiss the negative input, because the parents don't measure up either! The point of all this? Don't compare your persuadee to anyone or anything, unless the result of the comparison is that your persuadee seems swell in comparison.

INSIDER'S PLAYBOOK

Want something to look good? Pick a benchmark for something that looks bad, and make the comparison. Compared to that bad looking something, the good looking something will seem better than it is. Whether it's a house, a car, or a classic cigar, comparison helps people make important distinctions, as they differentiate one thing from another.

Want something to seem smart. Compare it to something dumb. Want something to seem affordable, or even cheap? Compare it to something expensive. But be warned. Too big of a comparison is hard to believe. Too small of a comparison is difficult to appreciate. You are after a meaningful AND believable comparison.

PRODUCT EXAMPLE: You can get the muscle tone of a 90-minute workout in 10 minutes!

SERVICE EXAMPLE: Instead of spending 30 to 40,000 on a solar system for your home, you can get a custom designed system with no system costs. Instead of dealing with permits on your own system, your custom system comes with no permit hassles.

IDEA EXAMPLE: You can read the words and listen to the audio program, and you will definitely recognize and learn a lot. Or you can use the activities in the Playbook to make what you're learning completely real to you. Which do you think is the better way to learn?

YOUR TURN: What can you compare your persuasion proposition to that increases the value of your proposition?

THE SIGNAL OF COMPARISON

CONSIDER THE ORDER OF COMPARISON

What do you want to leave in the mind of your persuadee? If it is fear, end with fear. If it is desire, end with desire.

You can also make a comparison by making two or three requests in a row. When a sequential request goes from large request to small, the small request seems much smaller and is more likely to get a 'Yes!' Or reveal the top of the line and then the bottom of the line, and the middle may have some appeal as the best of both worlds.

PRODUCT EXAMPLE: There are several models of vibrational exercisers. Here's one for $15,000. Too much? I understand. Here's one for $900. The motion is more jarring than jiggling, so it's hard on the joints. But the price is nice! Ours cost less than $3000, and has the affiliate program too.

SERVICE EXAMPLE: Are you willing to spend $30K to 40K on a custom designed solar system for your home? Once the permits are handled and you find someone to install it, you own the equipment! I wouldn't want to deal with the maintenance. Here's a system that you don't own. The company will custom design and install it for you, and you only pay for the service. As the cost of energy increases over the next 25 years, your rate is locked in from the moment you sign the agreement. It can never go higher. And if rates go lower, your rate will be adjusted to the lower level.

IDEA EXAMPLE: You could try to read the Playbook like a book, cover-to-cover, and think about the activities as you read. Better, I think, to use it the way it was written, as a self-guided self-paced program to get a superior result.

YOUR TURN: What benchmark can you use to make your comparison? What sequence can you use to make your proposition seem most persuasive?

INSIDER'S PLAYBOOK

IMPLIED COMPARISON

New and improved implies that the old one didn't work so well. Better, or faster, or more enjoyable, implies that something was worse, slower, and less enjoyable. Highlight the failures of the people or groups at the head of the old way of doing things and your proposed direction seems better in comparison. Highlight the failures of people or groups that have refused to conform and the old way of doing things seems better in comparison.

PRODUCT EXAMPLE: This V.E. model is greatly improved, with some fantastic enhancements. It is far superior to the low-end models, and offers you the best features of the high-end model.

SERVICE EXAMPLE: Finally, a way of bringing affordable solar energy to homeowners!

IDEA EXAMPLE: The Playbook is the most important part of the Insider's Guide program!

YOUR TURN: What words can you use to imply a comparison for your proposition without actually making the comparison?

THE SIGNAL OF COMPARISON

INVITE THE COMPARISON

When a comparison is too hard to follow, offers too many details to adequately consider, or requires too many assumptions on the part of your persuadee, instead of making the comparison, invite the comparison. An invitation includes a request. "If you put these two payment plans side by side, you will recognize that my plan offers more flexibility and payment options than my competitor. "If you compare these two products, you will notice that my product offers many benefits that the other product cannot." The beauty of this approach is that people will be more inclined to take your word than to make the comparison themselves.

PRODUCT EXAMPLE: Compare this model to either the high end or the low-end model, and you'll quickly discover just what an amazing value this is.

SERVICE EXAMPLE: If you compare the service model to the ownership model, you'll find that it's smarter, cheaper and in so many ways better than the owning the system.

IDEA EXAMPLE: If you compare the result of doing the activities in the Playbook to the results of simply hearing or reading the Insider's Guide, the difference in an individual's persuasive power will be quite apparent to you.

YOUR TURN:

HOW TO BE LESS PRONE TO COMPARISONS:

Keyword: **DEAL!**

When someone tries to take advantage of you by making comparisons, separate the items being compared one from the other and consider each on it's own.

PRODUCT EXAMPLE: What do I think of the cost/benefit of this product on its own merit?

SERVICE EXAMPLE: Considered on its own, what do I think of the value of a solar energy service for my home?

IDEA EXAMPLE: What is the value of doing exercises as a way of learning persuasion? What do I think of the Playbook as a standalone program?

20

THE SIGNAL OF CONFORMITY

People tend to do what other people are doing.

We want to be part of movements and forces greater than ourselves, and for good reason. Our ability to survive as individuals depends on our ability to work together and move together for the greater good. People don't often like to stick out their neck or be the first to try something. People tend to do what others are doing.

Big changes through conformity happen on a bell curve. Enough early adopters and the momentum begins to build. You don't need a full-scale movement to start a movement. You just need a few people to get on board. Find your allies; build a small group to get the ball rolling. Identify and cultivate early adopters. The more you bring on board at the outset, the more will join in as you move forward. No one wants to stick his or her neck out, and gamble on losing it. But they'll eagerly follow the crowd to find out what's going on or be part of the success that they expect as a result of their conformity. Get something started, and the rest will follow.

Most of the rest. You don't need to wait for the dummies and dinosaurs. They never get it. They never will.

INSIDER'S PLAYBOOK

POPULAR, TRENDY, AND PROVEN
He must be great, otherwise why would all those people have bought his book? The winner must be doing something right or he'd be a loser like the other guy. It must be funny, everyone's laughing. It must be a moving sermon, everyone's putting money in the hat. It must be a credible diet, everyone's following it. He must know what he's talking about, everyone is deferring to his judgment! Help people see, hear and think about your idea as part of a growing trend, a popular movement, or at the least, something that others have done successfully.

PRODUCT EXAMPLE: An anti-aging clinic in California has a room filled with vibrational exercisers running non-stop for three years. They get amazing results. Every doctor or business owner who puts one of these in his waiting room or lobby is amazed to find how eager people are to use it. And two out of every four people that come over to try ours wind up getting one of their own.

SERVICE EXAMPLE: This company is at the leading edge of an important trend. With the high price of energy, people are now actively seeking dual-purpose alternatives that help them control costs and stop the worsening of our environment. And as more and more people come on board, a real revolution is taking place thanks to this well thought out service model for powering homes with solar.

IDEA EXAMPLE: At least 40% of the people who have purchased the Insider's Guide To The Art Of Persuasion on my website have included the Playbook. That should tell you something about the high esteem in which people hold active learning over passive learning.

YOUR TURN: How can you make your proposition something that is popular, trendy, or has been done successfully by someone else?

THE SIGNAL OF CONFORMITY

HOW TO BE YOUR OWN PERSON:

Keywords: **GOING ALONG TO GET ALONG**

THINK FOR YOURSELF! Is it right for you? Use your own best judgment.

PRODUCT EXAMPLE: Do you need to protect your bone density and muscle tone as you get older?

SERVICE EXAMPLE: Is using a service that provides a solar system to power your house right for your?

IDEA EXAMPLE: Do you need guidance and support to act on what you're learning? Or can you figure it out yourself?

21

THE SIGNAL OF RECIPROCITY

DO UNTO OTHERS, THEY'LL DO UNTO YOU

Give a little, get a little, because giving a little invokes some degree of obligation. A favor implies that you are acting against your own interest. It implies that you're making a sacrifice of some kind. A sacrifice of time. Of money. Of energy. Of privacy. Of valuable information. Of property.

Guarantees invoke this too. A guarantee says "I'm taking all the risk, so you won't have to." And when you look out for other people's interests ahead of your own, they have a reciprocal tendency to look out for your interests in return.

Create this effect by offering something for nothing. The desire to accept a free gift is incredibly powerful, and invokes an obligation to do something in return.

CAUTION: It can be effective to create a string of obligations. But be warned. If obligation turns to guilt, people may avoid you in order to avoid feeling bad.

THE SIGNAL OF RECIPROCITY

PRODUCT EXAMPLE: Free samples. Free offers. Offer to bring a Vibrational Exerciser to your persuadee's office! Assure them it won't cost them anything, and that it's an easy way to find out if their employees have an interest in using it on break time, and how that effects the quality of their work. Or invite them to come over to your office and try it out. Let them know that you're busy, but that you think this is important enough to make some time for them.

SERVICE EXAMPLE: Group meetings with free refreshments to discuss the service. Invite people to share their concerns about the environment and the cost of energy, and listen really well, so they will listen really well when you begin your proposition.

IDEA EXAMPLE: As a favor to you, I did all the research, all the organizing, and took precious time away from my family to give you the book that you're holding in your hands. And all I'm asking of you is to use it.

YOUR TURN: How can you invoke some sense o f obligation around your persuasion proposition?

Concession-trading.

The trading of concessions leads to a negotiated outcome. Never make more than one concession at a time. Wait for the first one to be reciprocated before offering the next one.

How to protect yourself from reciprocity signals:

Keywords: **BEWARE A STRANGER BEARING GIFTS**

When an offer is extended to you, think! Open your eyes when a hand is extended to you. Ask yourself, would I have an interest in this if there wasn't something free or a favor or sacrifice attached. If someone really wants to give you something, let him. Since giving and receiving go hand in hand, and sometimes the greatest gift we can give is receiving another's gift, you can consider yourself even.

PRODUCT EXAMPLE: Would I be interested in V.E. if he didn't bring it to the office?

SERVICE EXAMPLE: Would I be interested in solar energy without the free refreshments and nice listening to my concerns?

IDEA EXAMPLE: Would I do the activities in the Playbook even if he didn't sacrifice all that time and energy to be away from his family, who misses him when he's working so hard, just to put this book in my hands?

If guilt is your problem, please consider reading my e-Book on 'Dealing With Relatives.' It makes the complexities of family relationships simple to understand and deal with, and covers a whole host of bad behavior, from criticism to meddling, from bossiness to bragging. And, more to the point, it contains a number of powerful strategies for staying off the guilt trips.

22

THE SIGNAL OF AUTHORITY

We are culturally conditioned to be obedient, we are taught that honor and duty go together, and we find reinforcement throughout our upbringing, in the form of rewards for obedience and punishment for defiance. The result: People will do what they are told to do, even if they think it is wrong, as long as the person telling them to do it is considered to be in a greater position of authority.

How do you project an air of authority? And how much of the signal do you send before it creates a backlash? You have between two seconds and two minutes before a first impression of you and your proposition is complete. And a first impression tends to be based on appearance, credentials, perceived experience, and the people with whom you associate, along with the authentic authority you convey in the way you talk and behave. A warning is in order here. Some people have trouble with authority. If all you have is authority, be prepared for resistance. People don't like to be talked down to, they don't care for arrogance and they resist any idea that they didn't think of first. Balance the authority signal with other persuasion signals in order to create true persuasive power.

INSIDER'S PLAYBOOK

THE APPEARANCE OF AUTHORITY

Professional presenters learn to dress a little nicer than their audience. Why? If you dress for success, you appear successful. Dress down from your audience, they are likely to feel superior to you, and give less credence to what you have to say. Is this always true? No. Some people feel more comfortable around comfortably dressed people. That's the value in knowing something about your persuadee before making personal contact. But in general, people respond to appearance and grant some authority to those who pay attention to it.

In clothing colors, dark implies authority and power. Navy blues and olives give the veneer of power. Black is so powerful that people who wear it may want to emphasize their affinity signals.

EXPERIENCE CONVEYS AUTHORITY

Speak from experience. Stand on your experience. Draw on the experience of your supporters. Experience implies tried and true, and a track record of learning, even if it isn't true!

ASSOCIATIONS CONVEY AUTHORITY

Others with authority can bestow some of their authority on you, so it is wise to cultivate relationships with opinion makers and king makers when possible. People who know the right people can have a strong front, because they know someone is watching their back. The size and quality of your network, the cumulative authority and experience it contains, may determine your future.

THE SIGNAL OF AUTHORITY

AUTHORITY BY DEGREES

People who have earned degrees have demonstrated a certain level of commitment, and people honor their achievement by granting it authority. A person with little education but much achievement will be granted authority for the same reason. The point? Point to your own commitment, history of follow through and achievement in order to send the authority signal.

PRODUCT EXAMPLE My reputation is the most valuable thing I have, and I would never put it as risk for a half-baked notion. I've thoroughly investigated this product to see if the claims made about it hold up to scrutiny. And indeed they do. As a doctor, I view this product as a real benefit to my patients. As a person, I recommend this product to my family and my friends. And the list of athletes and movie stars who are turning to this time saving exercise grows longer every day.

SERVICE EXAMPLE: There is no longer any debate in the scientific community regarding whether or not climate change is happening. It is. The only debate is long do we have before it is too late to change course. And there's still time. Study after study tells us that we have to change our lifestyle. And with this revolution in providing energy to households, we can do something that matters, and do it while there's still time.

IDEA EXAMPLE: My clients tell me that the material you're learning in the Playbook has helped them get promotions, build businesses, and engage communities in positive change. Don't take my word for it. I'm happy to provide you with copies of the letters and emails I receive regularly from people who have taken hold of their lives, learned to persuade, and used their skill to change their world.

YOUR TURN:

INSIDER'S PLAYBOOK

AUTHENTIC AUTHORITY

You don't need a degree to have authority. The authentic signal of authority gets sent in subtle and not-so-subtle ways. It begins inside you, with self-respect. Confidence conveys authority, and confidence comes from preparation. Confidence is expressed in the way you enter a room, begin to speak, the sound of your voice and the look on your face.

EVIDENCE AND TESTIMONY

No matter how persuasive your presentation, it's great to have great evidence and testimony to back it up.

Favorable evidence grants you authority, and unfavorable evidence undermines your authority. But it's not the quality of evidence that counts most, but the quantity of it. The more evidence you offer, the more authority you convey, because a lot of evidence is more persuasive than a little. The words 'Studies show' convey authority.

Having people testify on behalf of your proposition is useful when you don't have a lot of facts on your side. There are two kinds of testimony, EXPERT, and OTHER THAN YOU. The 'OTHER THAN YOU' testimony is particularly effective with children! Like with other evidence, sometimes it isn't about the quality of the testimony, but the amount of it.

MORE THAN ONE SIDE TO CONSIDER

If people are already inclined to support you, you can put the best case forward. If you know that your proposal will be met with opposition, provide evidence for and against your proposal, and characterize, undermine and refute the evidence against as you present it.

THE SIGNAL OF AUTHORITY

PRODUCT EXAMPLE: I can show you numerous studies that were done properly and by competent scientists wanting to know the effects of vibrational exercise on muscle tone, bone density and equilibrium. The evidence is clear from these studies. V.E. provides tangible benefits in each of these areas. You can see this research for yourself by visiting www.bevibrantandhealthy.com

SERVICE EXAMPLE: 71% of the U.S. energy market favors requiring power companies to generate at least 20% of their electricity from alternative renewable energy sources. And studies clearly demonstrate that solar power is an "immediate, viable, and sustainable solution to the energy challenges facing our nation." according to Rhone Resch, president of the Solar Energy Industries Association (SEIA.)

IDEA EXAMPLE: Dr. Jay Shoemaker recently wrote to tell me that The Insider's Guide To The Art Of Persuasion is making a tremendous difference in his work with his patients.

YOUR TURN: What evidence can you provide for your proposition? What kind of testimony?

BE CAREFUL!

Warning: "Studies show"

Keywords: **STUDIES, EVIDENCE**

Think for yourself.

PRODUCT EXAMPLE: Who did these studies? Did they stand to benefit from getting a particular result? (No they didn't. You can read them yourself at the website.)

SERVICE EXAMPLE: Are the people making these claims really experts? (Yes they are. Read about them and find out for yourself.)

IDEA EXAMPLE: Glad it's working for Dr. Shoemaker. Is his experience typical? (You are the best way to test that out. Finish the Playbook, and then send me your results!)

23

THE SIGNAL OF CONSISTENCY

CONSISTENCY FULFILLS EXPECTATIONS

When you give your word, it sets a level of expectation. When you keep it, you send the signal of consistency. If you keep it consistently, people come to expect you to be consistent. We associate consistency with character, with personal and intellectual strength. Products, services and ideas also must fulfill expectations in order to send the signal of consistency.

INCONSISTENCY LEADS TO DISSONANCE

If the value of a product you purchase is inconsistent with the price you pay, cognitive dissonance leads to a loss of trust. If promises are made and not kept, trust and credibility are lost.

Life is complex. Issues are complex. Decisions are complex. Consistency makes everything simpler. Once you've made a decision, made a commitment, or made up your mind, consistency means you don't have to think about it anymore. So most people would rather stick with a bad decision than have to admit to bad judgment! Most people hate dissonance. They ignore it. Avoid it. Deny it. Make excuses for it. Hope it goes away.

The only time dissonance persuades is when people draw the conclusion that change is necessary to restore consistency. If someone remains consistently inconsistent, they may in time successfully challenge a 'foolish consistency,' and bring about a positive change. But it's a far more difficult path than persuasion.

Personal consistency means that you treat people in such a way that they come to expect certain behaviors from you. That you know what you're talking about, because you do. That you are respectful, because you are.

Asking people to be consistent with their stated motivations and positions is powerfully persuasive. If someone tells you something they believe strongly in, and yet their choice violates that value, pointing out the inconsistency can be very persuasive. A person who claims to value family but spends no time with family may be moved to make great changes just by having this brought to his or her attention. A person who values health but doesn't get enough exercise may be moved to make great changes just by having this brought to his or her attention.

GET A COMMITMENT, ASK FOR CONSISTENCY

If you can persuade a person to say yes to your first request, they are increasingly likely, thanks to the desire for consistency, to say yes to your next request. If you can get a person to make a public commitment to an idea that you can use to support your proposition before you've offered your proposition, you are likely to be more persuasive with that person.

THE SIGNAL OF CONSISTENCY

PRODUCT EXAMPLE: You care about your health, right? Yes. What kind of life do you want to have in your senior years? Flexibility? Pain free? Strong bones? Good mobility and balance? Yes. Yes. Yes. Yes. But you just don't have much time to work out? No. What if I could show you a way to get those health results in very little time? Would that be of interest to you?

SERVICE EXAMPLE: Do you care much about the environment? Yes. Are you at all concerned about climate change? Yes. Does the fact that every time you drive a car, you could be funding a terrorist bother you? Yes. And you like to save money, right? Yes. If I could show you a way to stop funding terrorism, improve the environment, and save you money, would you be interested?

IDEA EXAMPLE: There's a good reason that you're interested in this subject, right? And being more persuasive is important to you? Can you think of a few times when you wish you would have been more persuasive? Do you think you'll ever have persuasion challenges again? Then doesn't it make sense to learn this material as deeply as possible, so it is engrained in your mind and available the next time you need it?

YOUR TURN: Obviously, being true to your word and acting consistently with your values, keeping your promises and agreements, all add to your persuasive power. But how can you add consistency to your persuasion proposition?

STAY SAFE

Warning: "Could you do this one little thing for me?"

Keywords: **SINCE, AFTER ALL**

When someone tries to get you to make a commitment, no matter how small, consider it carefully. It could be the first step on a road of consistent steps. And if you've already gone down the road by making a commitment, the question you need to ask is this. If I had known at the time I said yes what I know now, would I keep going down this road? If the answer is no, you have the choice to STOP! Turn around. If the answer is yes, then your consistency speaks well of your character, and of your personal and intellectual strength.

24

THE SIGNAL OF SCARCITY

PEOPLE VALUE WHAT IS SCARCE

More competition means more valuable, because the competition means there is less to go around. Less available usually means more valuable, whether people, things or intangibles like time, information and energy. When you don't have much time, you value your time more and so do others. More available usually means less valuable. That's how the best volunteers get used up. The more they take on, the more they are expected to do, and the more they do, the less it is appreciated. Except at the annual awards banquet, when people figure out that they better appreciate what they have or they might lose it. Which works out well for the awardees. Because easy rewards mean little. The best rewards are the hardest to get.

PRIVILEGE, EXCLUSIVE, UNIQUE, ONE OF A KIND

Privilege and exclusivity are persuasive, whether it's information, admission, or opportunity. There's something special about being special.
Scarcity has a language of its own

The language of scarcity is urgency and importance, privilege and prestige, prohibition and forbidden fruit. "Ends this

INSIDER'S PLAYBOOK

Friday!" "Five Days Only!" "The next 23 people." "Last chance!" "Don't miss out!" "Scandalous!" "Private Now Public" "First time ever!" "$1000 pizza, complete with caviar!" "Available exclusively at _" "Made exclusively for _" "Many are called but few are chosen." And simply, "Hurry."

How to send the scarcity signal

PRODUCT EXAMPLE: Make an appointment to discuss your product at a specific time and place, rather than talking about it at any time or place. Offer your persuadee the opportunity to be first, or give them exclusive rights to it. Or have a bonus that is exclusively for your customers. "The Jigglers are in such demand that they're now taking backorders. But if you order from me in the next 24 hours, I can promise you that the equipment will arrive no later than three weeks from today."

SERVICE EXAMPLE: Design and installation of your system is on a first come, first served basis. As you can imagine, there's incredible demand for this service. And the sooner you enter into an agreement to have a system designed for your home, the sooner you can lock in your rate.

IDEA EXAMPLE: The Change Artist Guild is an exclusive membership only group that I work with directly through my company. Members get access to exclusive teleconferences and private sessions at a discounted rate. The Guild is only interested in having members that are truly committed to being change artists, because our members are successful people who don't want to waste any time. If you have the desire for massive support in your career and life, and you have what it takes to finish the Playbook, contact me through the contact form on my website, and someone from the Guild will be in touch. But don't wait too long.

THE SIGNAL OF SCARCITY

YOUR TURN: Limited time. Limited opportunity. Limited resources. Special, and exclusive. How can you send the signal of scarcity in your persuasion proposition?

How to protect yourself from the scarcity signal

Think for yourself! Just because something is limited doesn't mean it's better. Just because something is rare, doesn't mean it is valuable. So if it weren't scarce, would it still be something you need or might find useful?

25

QUESTIONS? OBJECTIONS?

A question is an exciting indicator that a person is interested in your proposition. Your goal is to understand and then answer the question in order to engage and deepen that interest.

ALWAYS BACKTRACK BEFORE ANSWERING

Backtracking increases acceptance and gives you a second chance to hear the question and notice what information is missing.

EXAMPLE: I don't understand. How you can be so sure that your proposal will be the best choice under the circumstances?

YOUR TURN: Backtrack the main idea in the example. Then list every information gate in the question and what question you might ask to get that information.

QUESTIONS? OBJECTIONS?

NOTICE TIME AND ACCESS

The question may have a time element (past, present or future) and an accessing element (sight sound or feeling.) Incorporate these elements in your response.

EXAMPLE: When will someone show us just how this is going to work?
Time element is: (Circle one) Past   Present   Future
Accessing element is: (Circle one) Sight   Sound   Feeling

EXAMPLE: When did you say this was going to happen?
Time element is: (Circle one) Past   Present   Future
Accessing element is: (Circle one) Sight   Sound   Feeling

EXAMPLE: How do you feel we can handle the increase in business?
Time element is: (Circle one) Past   Present   Future
Accessing element is: (Circle one) Sight   Sound   Feeling

REFRAME AND ANSWER

If you can't ask questions of your questioner, then you have to guess the meaning. Rather than putting a lot of time and energy into 'figuring it out,' simply restate the question to which you have an answer, and then answer your own question. Then ask the questioner to affirm that you answered the question. "Does that answer that for you?" This will either gain acceptance or more information.

EXAMPLE: Someone in a meeting demands, "Where did you get your data?"
YOUR TURN: Reframe the question. What else could it mean?
HINT: (Where may refer to a person, place or thing. Data may refer to specific data, not the collective data.)

INSIDER'S PLAYBOOK

EXAMPLE: Someone in a meeting asks, "Has anybody ever complained to you about it?"

YOUR TURN: Reframe the question. What else could it mean? What else?

HINT: (Complaint may refer to something specific rather than general, and might mean something other than whining)

EXAMPLE:
Reflect the question back to the questioner.
 "How do you feel about it?" or "What are your thoughts?" or " How do you view this?"
If you don't know the answer, you can admit it

When you don't know the answer to a question, 3 options:
* Say, "I don't know." and then ask if anyone else does
* Say "I don't know," and offer to find out.
* Reframe the question, and answer the new question. "I think the question you're asking me is _____ and the answer is _____."

GET OTHERS INVOLVED

If you ever feel cornered by the way a question is asked, that's a great time to broaden the discussion. What could you say to get other people involved in answering the question?

YOUR TURN: List three ways to do this now.

If you feel undermined, be a pro and focus forward
Be professional. Appreciate their ' honesty.' Use the relevancy question to tie their question back to your main point. "When you say _____, what does that have to do with_____?"

QUESTIONS? OBJECTIONS?

DEAL WITH OBJECTIONS

The best ideas are often met with doubts and fears. Your proposition might create this result, or simply bring to the surface what was already there. A lack of objections may mean a lack of commitment and interest. An objection is a strong and often emotional request for more information. It may represent fears about conflict or complication, or doubt in what you're proposing, or even self-doubt about the ability to do what you are asking. Others may have the same concerns. Your goal with an objection is to address it with information in order to eliminate it.

However, if you can predict it, you can plan for it. If you know it's coming, you can introduce it first. And once you've heard an objection, you can incorporate it into your proposition for the next presentation, thus making it stronger and more persuasive.

Helpful Hints about what is behind most objections:

1. NOT ABOUT MONEY, ABOUT VALUE

Find out, "Expensive compared to what?" Then compare the benefits of your proposition versus the one of lesser cost.

Break the cost down into an 'amount per day,' or 'amount per week,' or 'amount per item' and compare that amount to something for which your persuadee already spends that kind of money

Add up the benefits and ask how much those benefits would be worth to your persuadee.

Remind your persuadee of statements they've previously made regarding their interests and motivations.

INSIDER'S PLAYBOOK

If the objection includes a comparison to something less expensive, simply agree about the price, but gently disagree about the value. Then build value by highlighting the benefits and advantages of your proposition.

YOUR TURN: What value objection might you be likely to hear? And how would you respond to it?

2. NOT ABOUT FEATURES, ABOUT BENEFITS

Persuasion decisions are made on benefits, not features. First, find out which feature is missing or being used as a point of reference. Then find out how it provides a benefit. Lastly, determine if the feature is necessary, and if so, why it is so important. If you can then demonstrate how a different feature provides the same benefit. Or point to a different feature that provides a more valuable benefit.

YOUR TURN: What feature objection might you be likely to hear? And how would you respond to it?

3. FEELINGS OF FEAR AND PROCRASTINATION

Feeling objections are not signals for more information. Instead, they indicate a need for handholding, patience and asking questions.

Identify with the objection. "I understand how you can feel that way. I had that concern myself. And what I discovered

QUESTIONS? OBJECTIONS?

was ....." and explain how you resolved the issue for yourself.

YOUR TURN: What feeling objection might you be likely to hear? And how would you respond to it?

4. HIGHER AUTHORITY MEANS DOUBTS

The best response is to agree that's it is a good idea to talk to someone about something so important. If possible, identify with it by letting them know that you also like to talk out big decisions. Then ask, and "What part of my proposition will you discuss with so and so?" Then speak to those doubts, and ask again for a decision in favor of or against.

Or, find out if the person you are talking with actually makes this decision. If not, you can ask to speak to the decision maker yourself. If your persuadee is the decision maker, just asking this question might be enough to get your persuadee to make the decision.

5. NOT THE TIME ABOUT DELAY OR DETAIL

'I don't have the time for this right now," your persuadee is either putting off having to think about it until you give up and go away, or there are some missing details that require more time and attention than your persuadee has available at the moment.   In either case, appreciate and acknowledge the importance of giving your proposal the attention it deserves. Then ask, "When is a better time?"

INSIDER'S PLAYBOOK

If the objection is that your proposal would take too much time to implement, find out how much time is wasted under the current system.

If the objection is that there isn't enough time to implement your proposal, that's a signal that more detail is needed about how it can work.

YOUR TURN: What time objection might you hear regarding your persuasion proposition? How would you respond to it?

STILL YOUR TURN: Write out an objection that you might hear when making your presentation. Work your way through it in a dialog form with the person making the objection (yes, put words in their mouth and then reply)

OBJECTION:

RESPONSE:
1. (Write how you would say thank you.)
2. (Information gate questions.)
3. (Why is it important to them?)
4. (How can you respond to the deeper interest?)

QUESTIONS? OBJECTIONS?

DO ANOTHER TURN:
Write out an objection that you might hear when making your presentation. Work your way through a dialog about it with the person making the objection.

OBJECTION:

RESPONSE:
1. (Write out a thank you.)
2. (Information gate questions.)
3. (Why is it important to them?)
4. (How can you respond to the deeper interest?)

BASIC RULE: DON'T LIE OR EXAGGERATE

If the facts don't support you, admit it, and then give other facts. If there are disadvantages to your proposal, admit to them honestly and then emphasize the advantages. Since there's no such thing as a perfect decision, help people make their best decision.
1. Thank the person who offered the objection.
2. Find out specifically what it is.
3. Find out what's behind it.
4. Provide information that speaks to the deeper interest.

26

DEALING WITH OPPOSITION

The biggest mistake that you can make when faced with opposition in a public forum is to turn the encounter into a confrontation. Here's a list of options to help you maintain your dignity and continue to send persuasion signals to the others in the room.

Option #1: IT'S NOT PERSONAL
Some people don't know how to ask for help, and some don't know how to receive it when offered. Repeat to yourself, "It's not personal." Then make a game of it, and tell yourself the opposite in the privacy of your own mind, while nodding your head as if you completely hear and understand.

YOUR TURN: What's the worst thing someone could say about you or your proposition? What will you do if someone says that?

Option #2: TAKE A BREAK
Call time out if you need it. Decide if this conversation would be better as a private interaction than a spectator sport.

OPPOSITION

OPTION #3: GET OTHERS INVOLVED
Bring in others who may have influence in the situation, or a stake in the outcome. You can either ask if anyone wants to say something, or go around the room and ask each person what they think about it. As soon as you get some support, point it out, offer to talk privately, and go forward.

OPTION #4: USE THE TACTFUL INTERRUPTION

Repeat his name or gender over and over and over again until you have his attention. Say "Sir. Sir. Sir," until he says "What?" Then, Thank him for his feedback, and firmly offer to let him have the last word. Tell him where and when that can happen. "Thank you for your feedback. You are welcome to stay and talk with me at the end of the meeting. Now, as I was saying..."

Or use the short form. Name or gender repeatedly until you hear "What?" at which point you just pick up where you left off before the interruption.

OPTION #5: GET CURIOUS

Ask yourself what this person really wants, or just ask the person directly, "When you say (backtrack what they've just said,) what is it that you want right now?"

OPTION #6: SOW SEEDS OF DOUBT

Sow a few seeds of doubt about one small detail in what was said to you, using the information gate questions. "You say that I don't know what I'm talking about. How do you know that I don't know what I'm talking about? How *would* you know if I did? "

OPTION #7: PLAY THE POLARITY

Agree with the person opposing you, and then take a position more extreme than theirs. She says, "It won't work." And you agree. "You're right. It won't work. Not even you could find a way to make it work." If the person opposing you is a contrarian, then the only way she can remain opposed to you is to flip to your position! "Oh yeah? It will work, and here's how!"

He says, "This is pointless." You reply, "Ok, you're right. For you, it's pointless. You aren't capable of finding the point of this." Don't be surprised if he flips around.

OPTION #8: COMMAND RESPECT

When dealing with people who are hostile and aggressive, it is imperative that you conduct yourself in such a way that they can't help but admire your self-possession and self-control in dealing with them. Take charge over your breathing first. Slow it down and drop it into your diaphragm area. Then plant your feet firmly on the ground and grow some roots. Think before you talk. Be direct and to the point. And use some of the skills that follow.

OPTION #9: MAKE THE COVERT OVERT

When someone is out to get you, they may attack you openly or covertly, to your face or behind your back. If the attack is based in sarcasm rather than information, odds are that you are dealing with someone who feels out of control, and who believes their best chance at having some control is to undermine your self-control.

To bring hidden agendas and grudges to the surface directly, backtrack the remark and ask for its relevance.

OPPOSITION

"We are discussing my proposal to do _____. What does (that) have to do with _____? Or you can repeat it back and then ask for the intention behind it. "When you say that, what are you really trying to say?"

This pattern makes covert behavior obvious to others, and very uncomfortable for the person engaging in it. Keep it up as long as you have to for the discomfort to build to an unacceptable level. If he decides to tell you what's really going on, listen, draw it out, say thank you, and tell him that next time to just come out with it directly. Don't be surprised if this person becomes one of your strongest allies.

Rule #1. DON'T BE A WIMP!

You know what it means.

YOUR TURN: Can you think of anyone who might oppose your proposition? Imagine the kind of opposition they might give you, and practice mentally rehearsing each of these responses until you find that matches your style and their behavior best. Confidence comes from preparation. If opposition is predictable, then go ahead. Predict it and plan for it.

27

RULES FOR MEETINGS

The best-case scenario for group discussions is that they are focused, not on personalities and bad behavior, but on ideas to be considered and outcomes to be achieved.

But groups consist of individuals with competing interests and hidden agendas. To make the best use of meetings and avoid the worst of people, establish ground rules at the outset of a meeting, and rotate leadership for holding the group accountable to those rules. Make sure the rules are visible to everyone at the meeting, and get consent from each person to abide by the rules.

If someone doesn't want to agree to the rules, rather than drawing them out on group time, acknowledge their independence, and remind them that the rules are for them too. Then use the relevancy question, what does that have to do with this, whenever the meeting starts going off track.

Rule #1: HOLD THE FOCUS
Begin meetings with the end in mind. Answer these three questions right off the bat.
1. What are we doing here?
2. Why are we doing it?
3. Why does it matter?

OPPOSITION

Rule #2: LISTEN WHEN OTHERS TALK
Each person is accountable for understanding everyone else, and asking questions rather than guessing is how you get to that understanding.

Rule #3: EVERYONE GETS A CHANCE TO TALK
Have a specific limit on the amount of time for any individual to speak, in order to give everyone a chance to speak on each topic.

Rule #4: FIND COMMON GROUND
In the face of disagreement, find out what you can agree on in order to contain the disagreement to something specific and resolvable.

Rule #5: CONSIDER MULTIPLE VIEWS
Consider all points of view offered in the meeting to be as valid as your own, and consider each point of view before settling on any one view in particular.

Rule #6: DISCUSS DIFFERENCES RESPECTFULLY
No hostile or insulting remarks. Talk to each other the way you want others to talk to you. Treat them with the same level of respect that you desire for yourself.

Rule #7: FIND THE GOOD
Temper criticism with a PMI evaluation. PMI stands for Plus, Minus, and Interesting. This is what I like about it. This is what I don't like about it. This is what I find interesting about it.

Rule #8: SOLUTIONS ARE BETTER THAN BLAME
Learn from the past, and then apply what you've learned to the future.

28

CLOSING

In sales parlance, a 'close' is when you complete the persuasion process and bring your persuadee to a moment of decision. Because of the desire to conserve mental energy whenever possible, the most common and easily made decision a person can make is 'I'll deal with this later.' And the most likely response to your request for a decision is the fear of making the wrong choice. A successful closing means one less thing for both of you, or all of you, to carry over into the future.

Closing carries a sense of finality with it. Closed. Over. Done. So it may be helpful to work your way to it with a series of smaller decisions, rather than jumping to the end. Step by step is a powerful method of persuasion.

We've discussed at length the value of open-ended questions in the listening phase of persuasion. At the closing end of your proposition, you use closed-ended questions that require either a yes or a no. Preferably, yes more than no. That means you have to know the answer is yes before you ask the question.

When asking for a yes, nod your head up and down to signify that a yes answer is the correct one. Verbally and nonverbally, this collection of behavior is called 'Building a Yes

CLOSING

Set.' A yes set creates momentum for a positive response to your final question, the one in which you ask for the decision. Once the decision is made, you can go back to open ended questions to get the details of what happens next, when it happens, where it happens, and how it happens.

BUILD A YES SET

Here is an example of a series of questions designed to get a YES response.

Do you feel that I have understood your needs and interests?

Did I address all of your concerns regarding this?

Do you have enough information to understand what this is?

Do you have enough information to understand how it works?

Do you understand how you will benefit from this?

Wouldn't you love to be receiving all these benefits right now?

Do you understand how this is able to produce these benefits?

If it works as I've said, is it a good choice for you?

YOUR TURN: Apply this specifically to your persuasion proposition. Identify 8 questions that go step by step towards a final question regarding the adoption or dismissal of your proposition.

What if you get a NO?

Don't keep wasting time on a losing proposition. Wrap it up and move on. Some will. Some won't. So what. Someone else is waiting.

What if you get a MAYBE?

You've missed something. Stop pressing forward and drop your agenda. Find the MAP, and then start building again.

The last question

Your last question begins with a summary of benefits, and other important information about any details, like prices, discounts, and timing. Then you ask for the agreement, or for the green light to proceed. Before asking the last question, recognize it is out of your control and detach from the result.

There are two ways to ask the last question. You an ask for a yes or no answer. OR, you can assume you have the YES answer you desire, and offer to act on it. This implies a question. Then smile, wait, and whatever happens, appreciate your successes in the process.

Put the logic in writing

Most decisions are made emotionally, and then logic is used to justify the decision after it's been made. Keep the decision alive after you walk away by writing down the details. This leaves your persuadee with a reminder of the evidence that justified the decision just made. As you write down the details, offer assurances and reminders of the benefits gained through their decision, and how appreciative you are for the agreement.

29

PRESENCE

Making a persuasion presentation can be fun and exciting. Or the prospect of it can be intimidating and produce a lot of anxiety. Where does the anxiety come from? It's part physical, and part psychological. The psychological aspect has to do with self-doubt and fear. The physical anxiety is a result of the psychological anxiety. But it's the physical part that people have the most trouble with, because it seems more obvious than it actually is.

"Fear is merely excitement without the breath." So said famed Gestalt therapist, Fritz Perls. That's exactly right. You don't have to overcome anxiety and nervousness. You just have to know how to work with it.

BREATHE LOW AND SLOW

There are three basic ways you can breathe. High and shallow, middle and regular, low and slow. High and shallow is the breathing of stress. Middle and regular is for going about your daily business. Low and slow breathing is the breathing of intentional relaxation. It involves your diaphragm, and pushes your stomach out when you inhale. This grounds you and connects you to yourself, and allows you to maximize the amount of oxygen getting in to your system.

INSIDER'S PLAYBOOK

PRACTICE TIME: Right now, place a couple of fingers on your diaphragm (about halfway between your nipples and your belly button!) Then breathe, and if you've involved your diaphragm correctly, it will push your fingers away from your body. Do this really slowly, counting up to 10 or even 20. Then let go. Do this before presenting your proposition, and you will find that as you gain control over your breathing, your hands, feet and voice tend to follow along.

PRESS FINGERS AND TOES

Press your first finger and thumb together as hard as you can to create a pressure point that draws your unconscious attention away from nervousness and into the point. Or squish your toes into the floor as hard as you can. When you stop pressing, your body will relax a little. Do it again, your body will relax a little more.

USE A SYMBOLIC GESTURE

Pick a gesture, identify what it means to you, build it, practice it, and use it. First, decide what it will be. A specific hand movement? Arm movement? Let movement? Head movement? Interact with an invisible prop?

YOUR TURN: PICK SOMETHING NOW

Next, plant your feet firmly on the ground. Bend your knees a little. Breathe low and slow. Relax your shoulders. Now, remember a time when you were excited, happy, confident and eager, and had all the time in the world. (This remembered experience does not have to have anything to do with your proposal or presentation.) Now, as you remember these feelings, make your symbolic gesture.

YOUR TURN: DO THIS NOW. Shake it off. REPEAT SEVERAL TIMES.

PRESENCE

Next, practice doing it in the imaginary future where and when you are giving your presentation!

YOUR TURN: Right now, imagine yourself doing this symbolic gesture just before your presentation and in front of your persuadee, and imagine having the experience of those great feelings while delivering your proposal. Enjoy it. Yes!

TALK TO YOURSELF

Instead of listening reactively to your own negative self-talk, practice speaking proactively to yourself about the pleasure you experience and the strength you have when speaking. Encouraging words do change physiological responses.

EXAMPLE: Say these four words to yourself, enthusiastically and convincingly. I CAN DO THIS!

Four simple methods to increase your persuasive presence. Breathing low and slow, pressing fingers and toes, using a symbolic gesture and talking positively to yourself about the one essential belief needed for you to be persuasive.

30

AND IN CONCLUSION

A great proposition ends with a solid conclusion. "I told you what I'd tell you, and then I told you. Now let me tell you what I told you." Review the main items and actions that will take place. Revisit the ideas and information you've shared together. Then leave them laughing, leave them crying, or leave them with a sense of wonder.

I began working on the Insider's Guide with an intense desire to better understand the world around me, and to find the tools needed to change it for the better. You, my reader, have gone the extra distance. You had the will to finish what you began. Now here we are at the next beginning, talking about a conclusion.

Some people spend their lives watching television. Others live in order to tell their vision. I try to do both. There are some fantastic magicians working their wonders on TV these days, and they remind me of how my work as a teacher in the art of persuasion began.

When I was in naturopathic medical school, a friend and I had the opportunity to work with a mentor who was exploring the leading edge of a then new frontier called mind/body medicine. As a result of what he taught us, I felt a responsibility to share what I had learned with my fellow students.

CONCLUSION

My friend and I offered a ten-week workshop. Thought I did not know it then, that was the first live performance of what became my speaking career. People called the class 'The Magic Workshop.' We called it "The Magical Nature of Communication' workshop. But no matter what anyone called it, it caught on. It opened eyes, ears and minds to the possibility of helping people change from the inside out.

It really didn't cost much to take that first workshop, about the same as my Insider's Guide Playbook costs now. But we had an unusual entrance requirement. If someone wanted to participate in the workshop, he or she had to demonstrate commitment by learning and performing a magic trick for us. This was long before I learned the words 'Get a deposit.' My thought at the time was that anyone willing to learn a magic trick to take the class would be committed enough to be a good student. I had no interest in working with people who had no real interest. That's still true to this day.

Since we asked it of our students, we required it of ourselves as well. In preparing that first class, I learned a few magic tricks of my own and practiced them until I could perform them to the wonder of an audience. And along the way, I learned a few things about magicians and magic tricks.

I learned that Magicians like being in on the trick. And they enjoy watching each other succeed with a truly spectacular and hard to understand illusion. Competent magicians understand that while a trick appears magical to the non-magician, to their peers it appears technical and logical (technological!)

Magicians also understand that the trick only appears magical to the non-magician if it works! And for a trick to work, there are two conditions. First, the magician doing the trick has to be good at it, and second, the audience cannot know how it's done. Ergo, sum, MAGIC! Magicians work really hard at learning to do a trick so that you can't see how it is done. And they never tell how the trick is done.

I see the art of persuasion, in fact all the arts of change, as a close match for magic metaphorically. The practice of the art involves something akin to learning and using a set of communication tricks. And once you get how it's done, persuasion loses some of its magic for you, becomes a bit more technical and logical. But from that point on, when people practice the art, you notice it.

I believe that for everything that is lost, something else is gained. While I lost some of the wonder by learning the trick, I have gained a deeper pleasure and satisfaction in those meaingful interactions that are less contrived and more connected. I wish the same for you.

You know the kind of interactions I'm referring to, right? Straight up, no messing around, honest to goodness authentic communication. The kind where people are curious to know each other at the deeper structure of their differences because of how interesting such things are.

I wonder if you can imagine what good things can happen in a world where people understand the basic tricks of persuasion and enjoy using them, and watch each other use and perfect the art. Where people can engage with each other out of respect and genuine interest. I'm curious if it has occurred to you that such good could be more amazing than watching magic tricks!

Because of your follow through, you've now gone deep into an understanding about how to practice the art of persuasion. Please stay tuned to my work. At some point in the not too distant future, I will offer to take you deeper still, and reveal the advanced tricks of persuasion. But that's for another day. Let today be the day where you change your mind, change your life, and change your world for the better!

Rick Kirschner, Summer of 2007

CONCLUSION

P.S. Learn more about the VIBRATIONAL EXERCISER!
www.BeVibrantAndHealthy.com

P.S.S. Learn more about the CitizenRe SOLAR SYSTEM
www.jointhesolution.com/raidantpower

BIBLIOGRAPHY

Cialdini, Robert B. <u>The Psychology of Influence.</u> New York: William Morrow & Co, 1993

Mills, Harry. <u>Artful Persuasion</u>, New York: AMACOM, 2000

Sprague, Jo and Stuart, Douglas. <u>The Speaker's Handbook,</u> Ft. Worth, TX: Hartcourt Brace & Company, 2000

Butterfield, Steve Booth. <u>Steve's Primer of Practical Influence</u>. Online. 3 March 2005. <http://www.healthyinfluence.com/Primer/primer.htm>

Techniques for Changing Minds. Online. 10 July 2006. <http://www.changingminds.org/techniques/techniques.htm>

Vorhaus, John. <u>The Comic Toolbox</u>. Los Angeles: Silman-James Press, 1994

Weissman, Jerry. <u>Presenting to Win</u>. New Jersey: FTPrentice Hall, 2003

ABOUT THE AUTHOR

Rick Kirschner is a respected faculty member of the Institute for Management Studies and an adjunct professor at Southwest College of Naturopathic Medicine (SCNM.edu). An Oregon-licensed naturopathic physician since 1981, Dr. Kirschner was in private practice from 1981-1987, and specialized in the treatment of stress disorders. From 1987-1992, he was one of only 15 presenters chosen by the Tom Peters Group to present the revolutionary 'In Search of Excellence' and 'Thriving On Chaos' training programs to businesses around the world.

Dr. Kirschner speaks to some of the world's best-known organizations, from Heineken to NASA to the Starbucks Coffee Company. He's fun, people relate to him, and he offers a palette of attitudes and behaviors that change lives, relationships and businesses for the better.

He is author or coauthor of 9 audio and video programs, including the bestselling "Dealing With Difficult People.' He is the coauthor of the international bestseller, "Dealing With People You Can't Stand: How To Bring Out The Best in People At Their Worst' (Brinkman and Kirschner, McGraw Hill.) Other books include Life By Design, Love Thy Customer, and Dealing With Relatives (e-Book, available at TheArtofChange.com webstore)

He's been interviewed on hundreds of radio and television programs, including CNBC, FOX and CBC. His ideas on communication and conflict resolution are found in numerous newspapers and magazines including USA Today, London Times, The Wall Street Journal and Executive Excellence.

Dr. Kirschner resides in Southern Oregon with his wife and cats.

ALSO AVAILABLE FROM THE ART OF CHANGE LLC

SPEECHES and TRAINING
In keynote speeches for association events, in seminars and training for Fortune 1000 companies, and for executive and management retreats; in venues ranging from conference halls to grand theaters to meeting rooms, Dr. Rick Kirschner offers a powerful approach to dealing with change that unlocks creativity, enhances communication and increases commitment. He is persuasive, purposeful, and his programs consistently bring out the best in people. Dr. Kirschner can customize a presentation that supports the theme and objectives of your event. Bring The Art of Change Skills for Life™ to your organization!

COACHING and COUNSELING
Dr. Kirschner is a ready partner for change in the midst of your busy life. Are you ready for a change in your life? Then let Dr. Rick Kirschner help you to master The Art of Change! Benefits include increased clarity and confidence, better communication, stronger motivation, and lowered stress

The Art of Change LLC
P.O. Box 896, Ashland, OR 97520
Please use the contact form on our website.

ENEWS
Don't get mad. Get help! The Art of Change ENEWS will give you insights into the why, how, and what you can do to change your life, your relationships, your work, and your world for the better! And it's absolutely free! You'll also get exclusive offers on books, audio and video programs by Dr. Kirschner. To subscribe, visit TheArtofChange.com

AUDIO PROGRAMS
Dealing With Difficult People
  1 hour CD of Rick's live presentation

Insider's Guide To The Art of Persuasion
  8 CD comprehensive audio program

Living Your Life By Design
  1 hour CD of Rick's live presentation

BOOKS
Dealing with People You Can't Stand
  (Brinkman and Kirschner, McGraw Hill, 2004)
  Bring out the best in people at their worst

Dealing With Relatives
  (Brinkman and Kirschner, e-Book)
  Your guide to successful family relationships

Life By Design
  (Kirschner and Brinkman, McGraw Hill 2002)
  A plan to bring out the best in yourself

Love Thy Customer
  (Brinkman and Kirschner, McGraw Hill 2006)
  Creating delight, preventing dissatisfaction

24 Lessons: Dealing With Difficult People
  (Brinkman and Kirschner, McGraw Hill 2006)

The Art of Change LLC offers skills for life in keynote speeches, teleconferences, private coaching, organizational training, facilitation, and information products for positive change. You're invited to visit www.TheArtofChange.com Read the blog, listen to the podcast, and subscribe to The Art of Change ENEWS.

www.ingramcontent.com/pod-product-compliance
Lightning Source LLC
Chambersburg PA
CBHW032255150426
43195CB00008BA/460